Self-Hypnosis

How to Be the Manager of Your Life

Ingibjörg Bernhöft
bernhoft@gmail.com
www.bernhoft.is

Self-Hypnosis:

How to Be the Manager of Your Life

Ingibjörg Bernhöft

ISBN: 978-9935-9087-6-6

First Printing

Table of Contents

Preface

Why are so many people using self-hypnosis?

To improve well-being, skills, and courage. To capture the attention and move it to where we want it. In this way, we can change our thoughts toward various things.

Self-hypnosis involves calming your body and mind or sharpening your attention. That way, you can get your mind to work with you to fix and improve what you want to change in your conduct or behavior.

In self-hypnosis, imagination plays a big role: visualizing what it is you want to achieve or get.
Self-hypnosis doesn't fix or heal everything, but it helps us focus on the solution and thus feel better in the situation we are in at any given time.

With it, you can achieve better results in your own life. This applies to all of us. No matter who we are or what we do, self-hypnosis always helps. Then, we are focusing our minds on what we want to get in our lives or what we want to see happen. We use our minds to get there.

When you go into self-hypnosis, see a very clear picture in your mind of how you want things and have as many details as possible.

It is possible to use all the senses—sight, hearing, touch, taste, and smell—if applicable. Then allow the image in your mind to influence what you want to change and how you want things to be. Always keep your suggestions and the picture in your mind positive and in the present tense.

There's nothing you can't work with in self-hypnosis, and this book teaches you how to create your own self-hypnosis script, read it into your phone, and then listen to it at your convenience. This way, you can adapt your self-hypnosis practice to your goals.

This applies to all aspects of the mind: reducing stress, getting rid of anxiety and fear, changing behavior, pain management, increasing concentration, increasing confidence, increasing happiness, health, anticipation, etc., and for all kinds of sports: running, golf, swimming, archery, shooting, diving, and much more.

Self-hypnosis helps you direct your thoughts where you want them.

It matters so much how we think; how we think about ourselves and how we talk to ourselves in our minds. When we want to change something, it starts in the mind and in our thoughts. It's all about you and your thoughts. We decide how we think.

So, once you have the recording of your self-hypnosis script, then you have to listen again and again because repetition is what matters. We are getting the mind to change our old habits and adopt new ones.

By using self-hypnosis over and over again, muscle memory is created, and that means increased results.

There are many different methods of self-hypnosis taught in this book, so you are sure to find a way that works for you and your goals.

Good luck to you.

Chapter 1

How Self-Hypnosis Has Helped People

Not being able to sleep is hard.
How do you sleep?

Case study for better sleep

"I don't sleep well. I fall asleep quite quickly, but then I wake up after about an hour and a half, and it's very hard for me to fall back to sleep," said a client who came to my office for hypnosis because he had such a hard time sleeping. "Then I start thinking too much and solving various issues and forget myself in my thoughts. Time moves on, and many hours pass, and I'm just tossing and turning in bed. Early in the morning, I fall asleep, and then it's only a few hours until I have to wake up to go to work. When I wake up, I'm still so tired, and it affects the whole day.

"This affects my mood and performance throughout the day because when I'm so sleepless, everything is much more difficult, and it takes longer to do things. Then I don't really enjoy what I'm doing.

"So, I decided to learn how to use self-hypnosis to find a way to sleep better.

"I have now used self-hypnosis to sleep better, and it works really well for me. I have been using a script that I recorded just for myself, which is about ten minutes long. I recorded it on my phone. Now, when I wake up after an hour and a half, I can listen to my recording and go back to sleep. I now wake up refreshed and full of energy every day, which, of course, makes the day much better and more enjoyable. I know that sleep is so important and is the basis of our health and our mind functioning properly."

Your body gets a chance to regenerate and repair what needs to be repaired while you sleep.

We also need to pay attention to what we eat and drink so that it does not disturb our sleep. (Too much coffee, soda, wine, etc...)

Sleep problems can be caused by various ailments, such as stress, fear, anxiety, pain, and worries. By calming your mind, letting go, and allowing yourself to be still, you can see a big difference in your general well-being. Self-hypnosis is a very good option here.

It's great to write a book that teaches people new ways to use self-hypnosis. This is useful for you in so many areas of life, and it's assuring to find out how self-hypnosis can help.

Consider in your mind what self-hypnosis could do for you. Put yourself in a position where you are using self-hypnosis to improve your well-being or abilities. It could be your sleep or even something else that you want to improve or change in your life.

Could you use self-hypnosis right away today?

What is the first thing you want to use self-hypnosis for? Use your imagination and visualize achieving your goals. How do you feel?

Why read this book?

In this book, I will share easy-to-learn ideas and exercises that will help you control your own mind.

I will teach you how to adapt a self-hypnosis script that works for you. There are many scripts at the back of the book, and you can adapt them to your thoughts and ideas and thus manage to direct your thoughts where you want.

Positive thinking

Self-hypnosis is so powerful, and imagination is the biggest factor. We visualize how we want things to be and work toward it. We are not thinking about what we do not want. That disturbs our minds.
I have adopted for myself the idea that everything always goes well in everything I am doing or about to do. Although things don't always go as planned. Then I set new positive goals, and life goes on.

I can choose how I want to think and how I want to imagine how everything that I am doing will turn out.

My self-hypnosis journey

In my self-hypnosis, I go on a journey in my mind.
I allow myself to go into relaxation and calm down in a place where I am not disturbed.
I visualize what I'm about to do.
I put an image in my mind of what I am going to do.
I see colors in the picture, hear sound if it's relevant, smell if it's relevant, taste if it's relevant, and try to make the picture as clear and enjoyable as I can.
Then, the subconscious mind, our mind, starts working toward this goal.
The mind always wants us to be successful in everything we do, but we need to tell our mind what it is that we want. Have clear goals and work toward them in a positive way.

It is so great to see the result.
Positivity calls for positivity; that is a fact.
It is best to see the positivity and be the manager of your life.

Hypnosis can affect anything that the mind controls.

A man with obsessive-compulsive disorder (OCD) came to my office for hypnosis. OCD is characterized by chronic, involuntary, and repetitive thoughts and behaviors.

His problem was that he had to wash his hands endlessly and take a shower several times a day because of his fear of germs. It affected his skin so much, and it was hurtful.
He was so afraid of germs and what they could do to him. He had difficulty communicating with people because of this, and so he preferred to be alone as much as possible.

It was taking over his life. These behaviors colored his entire daily life. It also took so much time away from the busy activities of the day. It became difficult for him to do his work.
All this was accompanied by great discomfort and shame at not being able to control the compulsions.

He had already looked for help in many places but had not received enough relief.

He came to my office for hypnosis a few times, and we got the subconscious to work with him to reduce these messages that were endlessly being sent to him (the compulsion).

He decided to make an agreement with the subconscious and OCD to give him a break for two hours a day, and he specified the time of day.
He used his imagination and visualized the compulsion, what it looks like, its colors, and its role.

The mind is so powerful and always wants you to feel good. Your mind is ready to work with you if you have a clear message and say what it is you want. Then, you can improve your well-being in so many ways.

The message to the OCD went well, and he extended the time off he got from these compulsions.

Between our sessions, he used self-hypnosis and continued to negotiate a release from these compulsions. It always got better and better, and the time he was free from them got longer.
Self-hypnosis helped a lot there.

The success gave us so much hope. There's great joy and freedom to not have to be under these compulsions all day, every day.

Today, he uses self-hypnosis and is in good touch with his mind and subconscious. The OCD is still there, but he can reduce this compulsion so significantly that it makes a big difference to him and makes his whole life a lot easier.

It's strange to be able to make a deal with yourself to change a habit or compulsion, but it can be done. And self-hypnosis is the way to do it. I have experienced it many times.

The dentist and the light

Sitting in the dentist's chair is not my daughter's favorite thing to do.

But she has found a solution for herself so that she feels comfortable. She uses self-hypnosis.

When she is sitting in the dentist's chair, she asks for a moment to calm down and get her mind where she wants it to be. It only takes a moment.

She uses her imagination and sees herself in her mind where she lies on a sunny beach and enjoys the sun and the warmth from the sun. The light above the dentist's chair is the sun.

She imagines the beach, the people there, and the sea, and she hears the waves and smells the sea. It is a wonderful feeling.

Now she is ready for an examination or correction and the dentist can start working.

She thinks this is a great way to feel comfortable in the dentist's chair. She has been doing this for years.

Maybe you can use this method the next time you have to go to the dentist's chair.

Public speaking is easy

Standing up in front of an audience and making a speech is one of the hardest things people do.

"My final exam is in three weeks, and I've stopped sleeping properly because I'm so nervous about having to present my final essay in front of a lot of people."

I was approached by a student from the University of Iceland who was going to take her final exam, and the thought alone was very burdensome. She had always done well in school, but when the spotlight was on her and she had to stand in front of a group of people and make her case, she had a completely paralyzing and uncomfortable feeling, and her heart pounded.

She wanted to feel comfortable in this situation and be sure that she would do well because she knew that she knew the material very well.

In hypnosis, we went over how the mind works and how she was able to change her mindset and allow herself to take new paths. She rewired her mind by getting her subconscious to allow her to visualize herself doing brilliantly on the exam.

Then she learned self-hypnosis and used it every day, right up until the exam. She did this to reset her mind and visualize taking the exam with great calmness and deliberation, where she was full of confidence and joy and enjoyed shining in the exam.
Through self-hypnosis, she was harnessing her focus, finding calm, and using her imagination to see herself in this situation where she does brilliantly.

When she went to her exam, there was excitement but not fear, and she was confident that everything would go well.

The exam went great, and she did extremely well, and she felt very good the whole time. She was so pleasantly surprised by how well she felt during the exam. She was delighted with her performance and plans to continue using self-hypnosis in many areas of her life.

Self-hypnosis itself can certainly help you get to grips with your challenges and what you want to change or improve in yourself.

Just read about the method in this book to improve and fix what you want to improve and fix in your life.

Hypnosis can help with all that the mind controls. The stories I will tell you will show you how powerful self-hypnosis is and how it helps people achieve their goals in various fields.

Experiment and let yourself see the results you will achieve using self-hypnosis.
You need to have a clear goal in mind to achieve success.
When you reprogram our mind. you have certain propositions in your minds that you want to achieve.
Let the imagination bring images to your mind and see you in the place you want to be.

Positive thoughts and suggestions that we give ourselves have a great influence on our thoughts and well-being.

Working on yourself is a lifelong process, but the main thing is to take the first step to your right path and thus achieve the desired results and goals.

Author of this book

My name is Ingibjörg Bernhöft. I am a registered nurse with an MS in strategy and management from the University of Iceland and a hypnosis trainer. I completed my hypnosis exam in 2011 with John Sellars, who came to Iceland from Scotland and taught hypnosis here.
I have worked in nursing all my life, and I believe that hypnosis and nursing are related because both are helping people to feel better.

I have been working with hypnosis since 2012 and have my own practice in Kópavogur. Many people come to me for hypnosis to change something in their lives or to get rid of something they no longer want to carry with them.

I travel abroad to hypnosis conferences every year and sometimes twice a year. At these conferences, I learn more and see what others in the world are doing to help people feel better. You can read more about me on my homepage at www.bernhoft.is
I teach self-hypnosis to anyone who wants to learn it when they come to me for general hypnosis.

Many people have stopped smoking with the help of hypnosis. I often receive emails from satisfied customers who say that it has been a long time (many years) since they quit smoking with the help of hypnosis, and they are extremely happy with themselves. They said:

"It was easier than I expected. I am very happy to have stopped smoking :-)"

"Good morning. Everything is going well with me. I have quit smoking, thanks to you."

"I thought that since my sister was able to quit smoking, so can I. And now I have stopped, and we are both so happy to be free from smoking. Thank you from the heart."

It's nice to get comments like these.

Hypnosis has helped many people master their sleep. I have done guided self-hypnosis on audio files that I have given to clients after their hypnosis session. They can listen to it when they are going to sleep or if they wake up in the night and want to go back to sleep quickly.

Audio files make it easy

I was contacted by a woman in Florida who was having a hard time sleeping.
Since there was a long distance between us, we chatted on the phone, and I sent her an audio file and asked her to try it and see how it would benefit her.

She dropped me a line a few days later:

"My dear Ingibjörg, thank you from the bottom of my heart for the shipment that proved so good for me, and I intend to use it often."

Another client said:

"It's amazing how much this has helped me. It is easier to fall asleep using the audio file, and I sleep well through the night. I told my son about this. Can I send him the audio file so he can try it, too?"

"My son has tried the audio file and is very happy. He can fall asleep and sleep much better. He didn't expect that this would result in anything :-) but he found a big difference!"

An introduction to self-hypnosis

Sleep is so necessary for us all, and there are many people who manage their sleep problems with the help of hypnosis and self-hypnosis.

Sleep habits change with age. Children and teenagers fall asleep more easily than older people and sleep through the night despite some disturbances in the environment.
With age, it seems that sleep becomes more relaxed, and many things in the environment start to disturb.

With hypnosis, you can block out sounds from the environment so that they do not disturb you when you are falling asleep and when you are actually asleep.

Self-hypnosis helps you shift your focus from what you don't want to what you want to see in life. Focus on what we want to get and achieve in our lives because what we pay attention to grows and prospers.

Self-hypnosis makes us more powerful in the areas of our life in which we want to improve
It's all about ourselves. Allow yourself to bring your attention to what you are passionate about and what you want to bring into your life.

Self-hypnosis is a very powerful tool for taking control of your own life.
To be the manager of your life, you must decide to be there.

Visualize how you want things to be.
Get your mind to work with you toward the goals you want to achieve.
Keep the idea positive and clear in your mind and use your imagination because it is the strongest force to achieve your goals, and your mind wants you to do well and to be your best.

Self-hypnosis can be used in many areas of life to:

Change behaviour
Change feelings
Change attitudes
Increase self-confidence
Develop new skills
Reduce stress
Reduce anxiety
Overcome habits such as smoking, etc.
Improve ability in sports
Reduce pain
Improve sleep
and so much more.

You can also use self-hypnosis to maintain inner peace, well-being, and self-confidence.

Chapter 2

Why Self-Hypnosis Works

In Chapter 1, we looked at how self-hypnosis has helped many people with all kinds of problems and challenges to get a handle on life.

In Chapter 2, we're looking at why self-hypnosis works and what it takes to get the best results.

Golf

How do you feel when you play golf?

He had played golf since childhood and loved to play. He played golf often with his dad as a child and teenager. He made a lot of progress in golf with each passing year. He won many victories both personally and in tournaments for his club.

Life goes on, and he went to high school, but golf was not played as much there as before. Studies took up most of his time. Still, golf was always at the top of his mind, and he went to the golf course as often as possible.

His handicap got higher and higher, and he found he wasn't as good as before.

The tee shots were always the most difficult for him. But the putts were also teasing him. It was harder to get as far as before, and the golf ball didn't always want to go in the right direction, and it really bothered him.

He didn't understand why it didn't work out better. He tried using all the old exercises that had worked so well when he was a child and teenager, but nothing was enough.

It wasn't a good feeling, and he knew deep down that it didn't have to be this way.

He knew all the rules and rhythms, but it was as if his body was not moving as expected. It just didn't listen to the message and simply made independent decisions.

He decided to do some self-work and better define what it was that he needed to change to do better. The methods he used were not giving him the results he was looking for.

Something more had to happen.
He realized that golf, like life, is as much a mental game as a physical one.

He decided to try new ways, and self-hypnosis was chosen.

He decided to adapt his self-hypnosis to what was bothering him. He felt that he needed to be more relaxed, to always go to the golf course with a positive outlook, and to be sure in his mind that now it would work out. He saw a picture in his mind where everything worked out.

It's supposed to be fun on the golf course. Golf is a fun sport and good exercise for the body. It is also a wonderful outdoor activity in a beautiful environment with fun companions—there are so many positive things about playing golf.

He consulted a hypnotist to learn how to use self-hypnosis. He went for two sessions and learned how hypnosis works and how he could use self-hypnosis. He learned not to put too much pressure on himself.

He learned to create his own self-hypnosis and put into it everything he wanted to achieve in golf:
calmness, joy, enjoying the moment, increased confidence, being present, and practicing gratitude.

He stopped berating himself after a bad shot and instead focused on the joy of the game.

He read his self-hypnosis script into his phone (instructions at the back of the book) and listened daily for one week to begin with. After using self-hypnosis for one week, he noticed a big difference and was doing much better on the golf course. The strokes got better and better the more he used self-hypnosis, and he started to see the joy in golf again. He used his imagination and visualized what he was going to do and how he would do it.

He found the problem, put the solution in a positive guise, and into his self-hypnosis.

By addressing internal obstacles, he was able to overcome his doubting thoughts.

Self-hypnosis involves clearly visualizing positive statements or suggestions that you want to bring into your life. See yourself very clearly as you have achieved your goals, and everything is going brilliantly.

Self-hypnosis usually works quickly, but repetition is always good. You need to listen to your self-hypnosis script over and over again to get your mind absolutely clear on how you want things to be.

Please use your own self-hypnosis to solve your problem. It's about setting your mind where you want it to be and allowing yourself to flourish. Self-hypnosis is a powerful way to allow yourself to feel better, and many people have had good results using it.

Confidence

She was always so shy and insecure with very little self-confidence; she felt left out, and that people didn't really see her. She wanted to attract as little attention as possible because she didn't feel good when attention was focused on her. She really felt that she was overlooked in various tasks at work, which she knew she was very capable of solving.

She found it unbearable to be so shy and have so little self-confidence because she was fully aware that she could do much more than she was already doing at work and in her everyday life.

Being very bright, it is easy for her to learn. She had and still has a good job, and she had a good chance of moving up in her career and getting a promotion if this eternal shyness didn't always interfere with her daily life.

Shyness and a lack of confidence held her back from various opportunities. She blushed just when someone looked at her, and then she was so ashamed for blushing. People who struggle with this find it more difficult to get into good positions in the workplace or excel in any way despite their skills and capacity. They don't trust themselves to see themselves in a new situation because of shyness. It takes confidence and well-being to flourish.

That's why she just thought it was best to keep a low profile. Best to just do her job, and then she would be left alone.

She was approached by a colleague, one of her few friends at work, who saw that she had much more to offer at work and in life in general.

"I can see that you can do much more than you are doing now at work. You can handle bigger projects than you are doing. And I see that shyness is bothering you a lot. You should study hypnosis, especially self-hypnosis. Then, you can take control and deal with the problems one at a time that are causing this shyness. With self-hypnosis, you can find new ways to flourish and get more joy out of what you do. You can also boost your self-confidence along the way, get rid of this weakness, and do what you want. Then you can find out why this shyness is there and use self-hypnosis to overcome it."

In this way, it would be possible to deal with one problem at a time (enhance communication with people, participate in discussions at work and at home, etc.) and get a handle on this problem that had been so overwhelming.

She could not imagine seeking help from a psychologist, hypnotist, or other professional. She went online and bought herself a self-hypnosis recording online. It was actually in English, but she is great at languages, so it was fine. She listened again and again and found that it did her good.
She learned what was said there and was then able to change the text, adapting it to her problems. Thus, she created her own self-hypnosis. She read the text into her smartphone and listened to herself.

Once she was in self-hypnosis, she realized that there were many factors that needed to be aligned so that she felt even better. She tackled one task at a time and then linked them together in her mind, and the results did not stop. She found a big difference, and it encouraged her to keep listening to newer and newer recordings that she made herself.

She felt that everything was starting to go better at work. She started chatting more with her colleagues. She began to feel so much better in situations she didn't feel comfortable in before.

She had her eye on a certain position that she was determined to apply for. She had joined a group at work and became involved in most of what happened there.

She told me that she was so happy with self-hypnosis to get rid of what has been disturbing her well-being for so long. She also told me that she plans to continue practicing self-hypnosis as part of her life.

It is so important when you are building up your confidence and changing or resetting your mind, to treat others with respect.
Many studies have shown that your attitude is 80 percent of your success, and 20 percent is what you know.
That's why it's so important when you're working toward your goal to let those around you feel good, too. There may be situations where this does not apply, but most of the time, it does.

What can you do to control your life and be your own manager or CEO?

In the back of this book, there are many scripts that you should look at and see if you can use as a basis for something that you want to deal with within your own life. Adapt these scripts to what you want to change and improve in your own mind.

It is the case that if you are clear about what you want and can visualize it very clearly in your mind, then the subconscious mind will quickly adapt it to your thoughts and desires. That way, you can allow yourself to feel your best all the time in all the situations that come to you and be in the place in your mind where you want to be.

Are you wondering if self-hypnosis will be beneficial for you?

Reading about things and then intending to implement them is not the same as actually implementing them. The conscious mind is often distracting. You must allow yourself to relax and allow the silence to come over your mind. Getting calm is a nice feeling. Let your subconscious work and fix what you want to fix. Keep in mind what you want to see happen. Keep it clear and distinct in your mind and let your mind work to make it happen. That's where the imagination helps the most.

Old habits can be stubborn. It is often difficult to silence the voice of doubt, the voice of existing concerns, and self-criticism. You must get past these doubts, this critical mind, to get into self-hypnosis. It is done by being in peace and quiet for a while. Then comes that calm feeling, as when you're going to sleep, and the stillness comes over you. That's where your subconscious works, adjusts, improves, and resets what you're telling your mind to do.

Is self-hypnosis safe?

Many people have misconceptions about what hypnosis is. Hypnosis has been portrayed in many ways in movies

that are not true depictions. That's why there are sometimes doubts that hypnosis and self-hypnosis are good options.
When attempting self-hypnosis for the first time, many people are not entirely sure how it works and enter the process with a degree of caution that can hold self-hypnosis back.

Those of you who have a hard time being calm and can hardly stay still for a while often have a hard time getting into self-hypnosis. This is just practice, and you have to keep trying. Practice makes perfect.

I've had a few people ask me if they could get stuck in hypnosis or lose control of their thoughts. There is no reason to support that because self-hypnosis is just like calming down, and we always do that when we go to sleep.

Reasons for not being able to relax

There can be several reasons why it is difficult to calm down and quiet your mind. Let's see some of them.

Six points that prevent people from getting calm and thus into self-hypnosis:

1. All kinds of thoughts come from all directions and disturb inner peace.

2. They don't know how to behave to calm down. They need practice.
3. Some people don't believe this can work.
4. Something in the environment disturbs. Maybe some noise or other inconvenience.
5. Negativity can disturb relaxation. Reasoning takes over, and it's hard to stop these thoughts or stop paying attention to them.
6. Afraid of forgetting something that you should be doing. Feels like you shouldn't be doing this.

Let's look at each point separately.

1. All kinds of thoughts come from all directions and disturb inner peace.

There is often so much going on in our minds as if there are countless thoughts that come all at once. You feel as if you must solve many problems at once, but of course, this is not the case. We only think one thought at a time, but sometimes, there are so many thoughts running through our minds at the same time. Then, it is good to be able to calm these thoughts and organize them so that only one thought at a time is dealt with and the issues are resolved peacefully in your own mind.

- Breathe deeply and allow yourself to feel the stillness and calmness that come with each inhalation.

- Exhale and feel that with each exhalation, you let the stress and problems of the day pass away from you.
- Visualize yourself in a peaceful place where you always feel comfortable: a favorite place in nature, at the beach, at home, by the pool, or wherever suits you.
- Talk to yourself to calm your mind.
  "I am safe and completely calm
- "It's so nice to relax for a while and renew my energy."
- "I can relax for a while and get rid of the stress."
- Visualize yourself lying outside in the sun and feeling the warmth of the sun. Hear the environment, hear the birds singing, hear the trees in the wind, hear people, hear the traffic, and enjoy being where you are.

2. They don't know how to behave to calm down. They need practice.

Many people find it difficult to relax. Some feel that they're cheating going into self-hypnosis.
In any case, there may be thoughts that need to be dealt with, and that's why it's better to just move on and not worry about it all.

Being calm and having peace of mind helps us to think more clearly, and thus, we do better in whatever we have to do.

How to get calm

- Do breathing exercises. Breathe in calmness, peace, and joy, and breathe out all that is disturbing. Use your imagination and visualize this as clearly as possible.
- Go for walks, and explore the surroundings, and purposefully enjoy the silence. Stop and look and allow yourself to be in peace and quiet in your mind.
- Write a journal. Remove worries from your mind. Write them down and keep them in your journal. Check again after a week, and the problem is often no longer a problem or has become much more manageable.
- Be thankful for what you can be thankful for. There may be many things in your life to be grateful for.
- Listen to relaxing music or nature sounds. Listening to the rain or the tides or birdsong can be very soothing. Just be there and take some time to enjoy it.
- Then, there are various guided meditations that help many and also yoga.

3. Some people don't believe this can work.

All kinds of misunderstandings go on. There are many kinds of hypnotisms shown in movies that people think are accurate, but they are not.

Stage hypnosis is also something that scares many people. But it has nothing to do with self-hypnosis. Stage hypnosis is entertainment and is subject to strict rules.

Someone who has never experienced hypnosis has a hard time seeing that self-hypnosis can help.

Hypnosis is simply relaxing the mind and allowing the subconscious to work with you to adjust and reset your thoughts. It is to pass by the critical mind and use your imagination.

Hypnosis is widely researched and has proven to be very effective in conditioning the mind. Self-hypnosis can help to reset behavior and abilities. Most people who try hypnosis and self-hypnosis the right way find good results.

4. Something in the environment that disturbs. Maybe some noise or other inconvenience.

- There can be a sound or noise that steals the attention, and thus, it is difficult to calm down.
- It may also be that the person is in a place where they are not safe and do not feel comfortable.

- You need to be in a good place where there are no distractions during the time of self-hypnosis. That's how it works best.
- It may be the temperature in the room that is disturbing. It may be too hot or too cold.
- There may be interference from animals or light.
- The seat or bench may not be comfortable, making it difficult to use self-hypnosis.

5. The critical mind can disturb relaxation. Reasoning takes over, and it's hard to stop these thoughts or stop paying attention to them.

Some have doubts that this works because they do not have proof in their minds. Sceptics are like:

"Why should this work?"
"Whose nonsense is this?"
"Do I think this can influence my mind
and change my habits or feelings?"
"I just don't understand this."

Some people have such strong reasoning, and if they can't see or prove something, it's hard for them to believe or understand.
But there is so much that exists that we cannot explain or see:

Love: Love exists, and it gives very deep and clear feelings and desires. We can't prove love or deal with it, but it's still there.

Gravity: We see its effects but cannot directly observe or feel the force from it.

Time: We cannot touch it or see it.

Memory: We use it constantly but cannot see it or measure it physically.

Feelings: Happiness, sadness, joy, anger, etc. They all exist but are not tangible physically.

It is necessary to get past this critical mind and find peace and relaxation so that the endless doubts leave the mind. Relaxation and visualizing what you are about to do makes all the difference. Use your imagination.
It is the key to achieving good self-hypnosis.

6. Afraid of forgetting something that you should be doing. Feels like you shouldn't be doing this.

Some people think that after self-hypnosis, they are not themselves and will not do tasks that they need to do.
Others feel that they have so much to do that is more important to attend to at this moment, and therefore, they postpone their self-hypnosis.

- It is very good to plan when you are going to spend time in self-hypnosis.
- You need calm and to be alone for ten to twenty minutes.
- It is possible to go into self-hypnosis just for a short time, so it should be possible to include this in the day's schedule if you want to.

You can influence how you feel. You are the manager of your life. No one can change your thoughts except yourself. You decide whether you have positive thoughts or negative thoughts. This book shows you how to change your thinking patterns for the better using self-hypnosis.

****

In the first chapter, I showed you how many people have changed their lives for the better by using self-hypnosis. But self-hypnosis must be practiced for it to work. If nothing is done except reading the book, nothing happens.
Then, you have the skills to use self-hypnosis, but you must get started and put self-hypnosis into the plan for the day. Have a clear idea of what you want to work on in your self-hypnosis that day. Imagination is the key to self-hypnosis and envisioning as clearly as possible. Paint the picture in your mind as colorful and as clearly as possible. Then the self-hypnosis goes even better. Use the scripts at the back of the book as a reference and

then adapt them to your situation and apply them to achieve the best results for you.

Speaking in front of people

He was very afraid of speaking in front of people. He had this feeling since childhood, and it was a very uncomfortable thought. He felt sweat breaking out when he had to give a speech. He refused many times to participate in presentations at work because he did not trust himself to stand in front of people there and speak. He tried all kinds of methods to overcome this problem. He attended courses and read various books on this subject. He sought professional help, but it only helped temporarily. This underlying anxiety kept reminding him of itself again and again, coming to the forefront of his mind.

He had not tried hypnosis and was thinking of trying that and using self-hypnosis.
He went to a hypnotist who helped him a lot, and he taught himself hypnosis to use daily for the next few weeks. He learned to use positive suggestions and shift his mind from problems to solutions, from negativity to positivity, and focus his mind on achieving sustained success. This is reprogramming his mind and seeing clearly in his mind how he wanted things to be. The subconscious mind is always open to change, but the mind must know what it is you want. He wanted to replace fear with confidence and success.

He thought self-hypnosis was very strange at first, but as he continued, little by little, he felt it was beginning to affect his well-being. He began to feel calmer and more composed, and the thought of speaking in front of a group of people did not cause as much anxiety as before.

One day, he was faced with a task at work that tested his ability to speak in front of people.
He let go, and he was quite surprised when it all worked out well.
He saw then that he had already overcome his problem and realized that with this method, he could readjust more things in his life and gain control over his life. The best part about it all, he said, was that he could do it himself.

Have you ever felt that feeling of not trusting yourself to speak in front of a large group of people?

Speaking before an audience is one of the hardest things to do. Many people find it difficult to stand up and just say their name. There is no need to feel this way.

It's great to be able to congratulate friends or relatives on their special day at a birthday party.

It's also great to be able to participate in discussions at work or in meetings despite having to stand up and speak.

It just takes practice, and anyone can do it.

It is possible to practice in the mind as below:

Visualize yourself speaking in front of people and flourishing through it and feeling good. Thus, self-hypnosis would appear to overcome the problem using positive mental images of success.

Anyone can speak in front of people if that is what is needed and what the person wants.
You can resolve or significantly reduce challenges.

It is very common:

- to have too little self-confidence and not be able to do many things that your mind has set itself to. Confidence is trusting yourself to do what you want to do.
- for people not to sleep well enough for some reason. Sleep is so important to maintain good health.
- to worry about yourself or others for whatever reason. This can be because of a health problem, sadness, addiction, communication, and many other things.

Hypnosis itself can help to resolve or significantly reduce these challenges or problems by finding ways to achieve peace of mind. You can find new ways to get out of your problem and allow yourself to find inner peace and quiet.

Self-Hypnosis technique

Now it's about time to learn self-hypnosis!

- Begin to reset your mind.
- Communicate clearly to your mind how you want things to be.
- Engage in positive thinking.
- Visualize clearly and colorfully where you have achieved your goals.

Your mind wants you to feel good and to be the manager of your life.
That is why it is very important to have a clear vision of the future and aim for it.

Questions I have been asked and answers I have given regarding self-hypnosis:

1. Are there many methods of self-hypnosis?

Yes, there are many ways that self-hypnosis can be used.
In this book, there are many techniques for self-hypnosis, but that is only a part of the techniques that can be used. There are nine scripts for self-hypnosis in

this book. And no one method is better than another. It simply depends on what is best for each person.

2. What does self-hypnosis do for me?

Self-hypnosis helps you shift your focus from what you don't want to what you want in life. It helps you focus on what you want to get or achieve. And remember that anything we give attention to grows and prospers.

Hypnosis itself makes us more powerful in the areas of life we want to improve. It's all about ourselves.

Allow yourself to bring your attention to what you are passionate about and what you want to bring into your life and grow there.

The main thing is to be able to relax and allow your imagination and subconscious to work with you toward your goals.

Visualize the success as clearly as you can and feel the success within you sooner.
Then, the subconscious mind knows how you want things to be, and changes will begin to happen within you.

3. What can self-hypnosis be used for?

Self-hypnosis can be used for:

- Increasing confidence and developing new skills.
- Reducing stress and anxiety.
- Helping people overcome old habits that are no longer suitable for them.
- Overcoming bad habits such as smoking, biting nails, etc.
- Improving sleeping habits, getting rid of fears, etc.

You can use self-hypnosis to change or adjust your thoughts or behavior or to start doing something you have not trusted yourself to do before. Remember, we can only change ourselves.

Self-hypnosis is widely used by athletes to enhance their performance in sports.

4. Why is self-hypnosis a good option?

Self-hypnosis is a very safe technique that can bring us confidence, boldness, and relaxation.

Hypnosis itself can change our behavior, feelings, and attitudes, and self-hypnosis can increase confidence and happiness. We can develop new skills and new habits through self-hypnosis.

5. How long does it take to go into self-hypnosis?

It takes a short time to get into self-hypnosis. You need to be alone for a while and calm your mind. Then you can start working with the goal and the suggestions that you planned to work with in these self-hypnosis sessions. Most of the time, self-hypnosis takes 10 to 15 minutes. But it can be shorter, and it can be longer. It's very individual.

6. Does self-hypnosis give good results?

Yes, studies show that the results are very good for many people (Rees, 2023).
Self-hypnosis needs to be used properly, though, and if practiced regularly, the results will always be better and better.

For good results:

- It is necessary to prepare for self-hypnosis.
- Have a clear goal in mind.
- Visualize the results as vividly as possible.
- Use your imagination to find the best way.
- Write down positive affirmations/suggestions to use in self-hypnosis.

7. Is special preparation required for self-hypnosis?

It is always good to prepare well to achieve good results.

Here are the best ways to prepare:

Have a specific goal in mind.
Decide in advance how much time you will allow for self-hypnosis.
Make yourself as comfortable as you can before hypnotizing yourself.
Find a place where you feel comfortable and will not be disturbed.
Keep the goal/s clear in your mind that you are going to work on in this self-hypnosis.
Create positive affirmations/suggestions about your goals.
Write down the goals and affirmations you plan to keep in mind during the hypnosis session.
Keep all statements or suggestions positive.
Write down what you want to master.
What will achieving these goals change for you?
Relax your mind by letting your mind wander.
Breathe deeply and visualize yourself in deep relaxation.
Determine the place, time, and duration of the hypnosis itself.
Write down the goals that you are going to work toward in this hypnosis.

Write down positive suggestions that match your goals. Find positivity toward yourself and the conviction that you can do what you want.
Allow your imagination to come up with images of you where everything is going really well as you look ahead.

8. Can scripts be used for self-hypnosis?

Yes, you can use a script.
You can create your own or use the scripts that are in this book.
You can also edit the scripts in this book.
You can read and record the script into your phone, etc., and listen back to it.
Then, you can learn the script and carry it in your mind.
You can learn cues, so you know in which order to work.
You can also learn the introduction and deepening, then open your eyes and read from the paper that you wrote.
Then close your eyes, go back into deep relaxation, and allow your mind to process it all.

You can also listen to recordings from others that are suitable for you and your goals.
Hypnosis recordings are available at many sites on the internet.

At the back of this book, there are good explanations of the structure of hypnosis and clear instructions to follow when you want to create your own self-hypnosis session.
There are also instructions at the back of the book on

how you can record your self-hypnosis on your phone so you can listen to it when you practice self-hypnosis.

9. Do I need to have a recording that I make myself to be able to use self-hypnosis?

No, not at all. You can have written points on paper about what you are going to work on in your self-hypnosis session. It starts with being calm, then opening your eyes and reading from the paper. Then, close your eyes again and allow your mind to work with you on a solution.
More explanations will be given later in the book.

10. Can old age prevent me from achieving success when I use self-hypnosis?

No, absolutely not. If you want to use self-hypnosis, you can. Both young and old have used this method with good results.

When reprogramming the mind, we have certain propositions in mind of something we want to achieve.

Positive thoughts and suggestions that we give ourselves have a great influence on our thoughts and well-being.

We allow our imagination to bring images to the mind and see us in the place we want to be.

Working on yourself is a lifelong process, but the main thing is to take the first step and thus achieve the desired result and goals.

Chapter 3

What's the Difference between Hypnosis and Self-Hypnosis?

In fact, all hypnosis is self-hypnosis because no one controls our minds but ourselves. When we listen to something and follow the instructions, we are making the decision to follow the instructions. In hypnosis, we call these instructions "suggestions."

The mind is so powerful, and we can harness it where we want it to be.

Hypnosis is a natural state of mind where attention and concentration become sharper, and we find peace and quiet in the mind. In hypnosis, this calmness is like the calmness that comes over us just before we fall asleep.

When we come back from sleep to wakefulness, we go through this state of mind again.

We also feel this stillness and calmness when we sit in a chair and are almost asleep but still awake, then we are in a hypnotic state. Then, our brain waves are theta or alpha (see further for an explanation of brain waves). When the mind is occupied with something, and we forget ourselves for a while, the mind is in a hypnotic state.

This can apply to any kind of experience or work when you forget about yourself, and the imagination takes over.

Examples:

We are learning something and forget ourselves, and hours can pass in complete flow.

We are watching a movie, and we are inside the movie, experiencing what we are watching. We know for sure that we are watching a movie. We even know the actors and the plot, but still, we experience the film as if we were there taking part in the story.

We are on a walk somewhere and got into a certain state of mind, we forget ourselves on the walk and enjoy the moment and the beautiful surroundings
We are in our own mental world. We are immersed in daydreams.

Also, when the imagination is busy thinking about something, we see things clearly in pictures and colors and all the things our senses can allow us to experience. This also happens when we are driving. The mind drifts away from us, yet we are aware of what is happening and where we are going. We are fully prepared if we need to act. We just can't talk about everything we drove past on the way, but we were still aware and mindful of the drive. This is known as being on "autopilot." All this is a hypnotic state. This activity can be seen on an EEG. It is possible to see which brain waves are working in the mind at any given time.

Brain waves

There is a lot of electrical activity going on in the brain. That's because the cells in the brain called neurons use electrical impulses to communicate with each other.

When a group of neurons sends electrical impulses to another group of neurons, we call them brain waves. An electroencephalogram (EEG) test detects and measures the electrical activity in the brain, essentially creating an image that looks like a wave pattern that can then be read.

Brain waves have different activity throughout various times of the day depending on what we are doing at any given time. Brain waves move at different speeds—some brain waves are slower, others are faster. The measurement of the movement of brain waves is measured by Hz frequency.

Brain waves are divided into five categories according to the frequency of oscillation:
gamma, beta, alpha, theta and theta, each has a specific Hz frequency.

There is always electrical activity going on in the brain, whether we are aware of it or not.

Gamma brain waves range from 35–100 Hz. They are the fastest brain waves. Gamma waves are seen during intense mental activity when we perceive objects and when we are wide awake. Your brain produces gamma waves when you are very focused or active in solving a problem. Gamma waves help you process information.

Beta waves range from 13–30 Hz. They are associated with a normal state of alertness and good alertness, logic, and critical thinking. Beta brain waves are important for the effective functioning of the mind throughout the day.

Alpha waves range from 8–12 Hz. They give the feeling of calmness and of increased creativity, and when alpha waves are present, there is an increased ability to receive new information.

Hypnosis, meditation, and practicing mindfulness are some of the good ways to stay in the Alpha state. When you are awake, calm, and meditative, the alpha waves increase. Alpha brain waves occur best when we are relaxed and calm and when we close our eyes and relax. They are believed to be able to heal the body and soul.

You don't have to close your eyes to get into hypnosis; just be calm to reach an Alpha state of mind.

Theta waves range from 4–8 Hz. They are seen in people under hypnosis and in people in a trance state. Also, when people are daydreaming or during very shallow sleep. These waves are also seen just before sleep and when you are coming from sleep to wakefulness.

They are very common in children between the ages of two and six years during the day when they are playing creative games and activating their creativity. At this age, the critical mind has not developed. (More on this later.)

Delta waves range from 0.5–4 Hz. Deep, dreamless sleep produces delta waves. These waves are low and slow.

Conscious and Subconscious

The mind is divided into conscious and subconscious. The conscious mind is about 10 percent of our thoughts, and the subconscious mind is 90 percent.

The conscious mind controls everything we do consciously. The conscious mind also manages all our reasoning, all our planning, and all our decisions.

The subconscious mind manages everything that is unconscious—all that we don't have to think about when we execute. All the activities of the body from A–Z. Everything we have experienced. Everything we have learned so well that we don't have to think much to implement and all our manners and habits.

The subconscious mind is like a computer that stores all the information for us. It keeps everything we have done, learned, and experienced. We can then access these memories when convenient. Sometimes, we approach these memories consciously, sometimes we don't remember them completely, and need to recall them, but sometimes they come to mind when we are in a certain situation. These can be either good or bad memories.

Our perceptions, such as sight, hearing, touch, taste, and smell, can trigger memories.

We see something, and then we remember an incident. We hear something, and an image from the past comes to mind.
And so, it is with all our senses. They evoke memories and skills.
The critical mind is like the gatekeeper or filter between the conscious and the subconscious.

You are in a conversation, and in order for you to answer questions you're asked, questions like this come to mind: "How do I want to answer this?" The doorman comes in with questions because the critical mind is watching out for us. A question comes to you, and you think: Do I want this, or do I not want this? This is so that we use reason to make decisions. The mind wants us to be aware of what we want and what we don't want. The critical mind takes care of it.

Think of a glass of water. You can see the water line at the top of the glass. Think of the area above the surface of the water as the consciousness 10 percent. Below the water level, the subconscious is 90 percent. The line that separates the conscious and subconscious is called the critical mind.

The critical mind matures and starts to protect us when we are about six or seven years old. Until that time, the critical mind is not stopping us and asking questions. That's why children are so wonderfully open and love adventure stories. The stories become vivid in their minds, and they completely immerse themselves.

It is possible to induce a hypnotic state with certain methods, and the most common is to induce calmness and deliberation. In this way, it is possible to feel the theta or alpha waves and get the subconscious to work with us to change what we want to change or fix.

Hypnosis is when one hypnotizes another and the client listen to what hypnotist is saying, and it is based on the pre-interview before the hypnosis session.
Self-hypnosis is when we put ourselves in this state of mind through certain exercises or techniques .

In hypnosis, we bypass the critical mind and get the subconscious to try new ways to achieve the results we want to achieve. We stop being always on guard and stop overthinking things. We just allow the mind to work toward the goal we set and then see what comes out of it.

It's all about what we want ourselves. No one can control our mind but ourselves. That is why it is said that all hypnosis is self-hypnosis.

Self-hypnosis is called various other names, such as medical hypnosis, visualizing in the mind, or deep relaxation. In English, there are many names for self-hypnosis.

What are suggestions, and how can we use them?

Suggestions are phrases that we say to ourselves in self-hypnosis to remind us of how we want things to be. It's a behavior or thought you want to work on.

Suggestions are used to induce changes in our mind for perceptions, feelings, or behaviors.

Make all your suggestions positive.

Suggestions are divided into direct and indirect suggestions.

When we are creating our suggestions, we are talking to ourselves. We are calling to ourselves something that we want to achieve. It can be something objective or subjective.
We allow the mind to go inward to that deep unconscious part of the subconscious. We get the mind to engage in an internal dialogue and ask the subconscious to guide us to our goals.
There, we use intuition.

We do not point out what we don't want. We don't say in our minds, I don't want this, and I don't want that. Instead, our thinking needs to go to what we want, to what we think. The mind needs to be clear about where we are headed and what we want. Visualize this clearly in your mind. The subconscious perceives everything we think. We need to use positivity and love. Then, the subconscious is ready to take us to our goals.
We can change our thoughts, and we can activate our minds. The mind is energy, and we can harness our inner energy and direct the mind to where we want it to be. Isn't this amazing?

Remember that the suggestions must be in the present tense and positive.

Direct suggestions are direct statements that are ordinary and obvious and are often used in self-hypnosis.

For example:

The goal is:
I want to fall asleep easily.
The suggestion could be:
"I can sleep easily now."

The goal is:
I want to be smoke-free and be happy about it.
The suggestion could be:
"I'm completely smoke-free, and I'm so happy about it."

The goal is:
I want to feel safe in everything I do.
The suggestion could be:
"I am confident and capable in everything I do."

The goal is:
I want to feel calm inside and feel good.
The suggestion could be:
"I'm relaxed and feel better and better every day."

The goal is:
I want to be able to move more and feel my energy increase.
The suggestion could be:
"Every day I walk for fifteen minutes and feel the energy coming to me, and I am so proud of myself."
The goal is:
I want to manage to find inner peace.
The suggestion could be:

"I take a deep breath, and when I exhale, I completely relax."

The goal is:
I want to be able to close my eyes and find inner peace.
The suggestion could be:
"My eyelids are heavy over my eyes and it's so soothing."

The goal is:
I want to be able to wake up refreshed in the morning and have lots of energy.
The suggestion could be:
"When I wake up in the morning, I am refreshed and full of energy."

They are like direct convictions, very clear propositions, said straightforwardly.

Indirect suggestions
They are not commanding or controlling.

For example:

"I may feel that my hands and feet are heavy or light."

"I wonder if I can feel the relaxation spread throughout my body."
"I may feel that my right hand is heavy or light, and I wonder if I can feel the relaxation spreading up my arm."

"I wonder if I can see myself where I sleep a sweet, nourishing sleep and where I can sleep through the night?"

Milton Erickson the American psychiatrist and psychologist was very well known for his family therapies due to his use of hypnosis in his treatments, He used indirect suggestions a lot.

Considered the father of modern hypnosis, he developed techniques known as Ericksonian Hypnosis. He didn't use commands. He used implicit suggestions that were incorporated into all the stories he used in his therapy. He also used metaphors or casual dialogue.

For example:

"When you relax, you may feel a great sense of relaxation come over you, and you may feel that you are freed from the stress that has been bothering you."

"Why don't you rest for a while?"

"Many people experience a calming atmosphere here."

"The sound of the water can be so soothing."

"You may find that you are much more relaxed now."

"You may notice that .... "

When to use direct suggestions and when to use indirect suggestions?

Chapter 4

To Hypnotize Oneself

Self-hypnosis refers to when a person enters a hypnotic state by themselves without any outside help. Anyone can induce this pleasant state and use it to maximize their performance.

Self-hypnosis is like normal hypnosis, except you are hypnotizing yourself.

This technique is based on skill, knowledge, and practice, and once you learn it, you can help yourself in many ways.

Self-hypnosis is a natural state that we go through many times a day:

- Whenever we are on the way into sleep and when we wake up.
- Whenever we forget about ourselves during tasks.

- Whenever we are daydreaming.
- Whenever we are absorbed in thoughts or activities.
- Whenever we allow ourselves to relax and be still.

Can I work with multiple issues/challenges in one self-hypnosis session?

It is recommended to only address one problem or challenge at a time in self-help unless they are related.

Self-hypnosis can:

- Help you improve in sports and increase your self-confidence.
- Get rid of stress and help you to find inner calm and peace.
- Reduce anxiety and help you to feel at ease.
- Quit smoking and help you to find the freedom and joy within.
- Reduce pain and help you to feel that you can move better.

What is the best preparation for self-hypnosis?

Practicing being still and being still for two minutes while doing nothing.
Let your mind wander, and don't control it.
Just follow your thoughts and let them float past you. They are just thoughts.

Find a certain place where you can go into self-hypnosis and be in peace and quiet for ten to fifteen minutes.
Be sure to decide in advance what you are going to work on in your self-hypnosis session.
Write it on a piece of paper and keep it with you.

(It's good to write down how you feel when the goal is reached. What does that mean to you?)

During your self-hypnosis practice, use your imagination to visualize your goal as clearly as possible with picture, color, and sound, and maybe smell and taste if they are relevant.

How do we perform self-hypnosis?

- Find a quiet place.
- Sit down in a comfortable chair, sofa, or bed. Some prefer to lie down, but then there is a greater risk of falling asleep!
- Place your feet on the floor and your hands on the arms of your chair or in your lap.
- You will be in this position for some time, so it is more comfortable not to cross your legs.
- Have a specific goal in mind for the self-hypnosis.
- Allow yourself to be in the present, here and now.
- Listen to what your subconscious mind is telling you.
- Ask your mind questions and get answers.
- Listen to your mind.

- It is best to have only one goal to work on in self-hypnosis or two related ones.
- Let your imagination take over.
- Turn off your phone, computer, and anything else that might make noise or disturb you during your self-hypnosis.
- Find peace within and allow relaxation to come to you.
- You can keep your eyes open or closed as you wish.

There are scripts in this book with clear instructions for the entire self-hypnosis technique.

The Steps: An explanation of how this works

- Find a quiet place where you feel comfortable and won't be disturbed.
- It is best to sit in a good chair with your feet on the floor and your hands on the arm of the chair or in your lap.
- Visualize how you want things to be.
- Close your eyes and allow the stillness and calm to come to you.
- Take a deep breath and allow calm and pleasantness to come with the inhalation.
- Breathe out and let all the stress and distractions of the day go with the exhale. Clear your mind as much as possible.

- If thoughts come, see them, but don't judge anything, and let them pass you by. These are just thoughts.
- Notice tension in your body and allow it to pass away.
- Bring to mind a place in your body where you feel good. Allow that feeling to spread throughout your body.
- Then begin to relax your entire body from the top of your head down to the tips of your toes.
- Or start the relaxation on the toes and move up along the body and to the vortex.
- Relax well in each area separately.

And to go deeper into self-hypnosis and relaxation:

- Visualize a staircase in a beautiful place in your mind. The staircase has ten steps, and you are going down them. Then you will come to a beautiful place that is there below the stairs. With each step you take down the stairs, you always go deeper and deeper into relaxation. When you have come down all the stairs, you are completely relaxed and feel very good. We call this place the Peaceful Place, the Quality place, or just the Safe Place. Allow your attention to be there, and allow yourself to feel comfortable there, whether you are sitting or lying down. Visualize this clearly in your mind. Here, you could open your eyes and read your statement or the suggestions you decided to use in this self-hypnosis. Visualize yourself where you have achieved your goals and are the winner.

- Repeat the statements (suggestions) several times.
- Then close your eyes again and give your mind a moment to process this and adjust what is needed. You will know how much time you need.
- When you are comfortable with what you are doing, you can get your subconscious to increase your confidence and well-being or whatever else suits you.
- When you are ready to come back from self-hypnosis, you either just open your eyes or count 1 2 3 4 5.
- Open your eyes, be fully awake, and feel wonderful. You will feel refreshed, rejuvenated, and have a lot of energy.

How can I record self-hypnosis on my smartphone?

Recording using your iPhone

How to stop incoming calls while recording audio on your iPhone:

Go to Settings
Then Focus
and Do Not Disturb

Select People

Then you will see Silence Notification From. This should be off.
There is also an Allow Notification From. Check that it's on.

Click Allow Calls From (click at the end of that line)
Select Allow People Only
At the bottom of the screen:
Allow Repeated Calls Choose this, as when selected, it works as a backup so that you can be reached if necessary.

If someone calls you and you have the phone on Do Not Disturb because you are recording, but it is urgent to reach you, then the relevant number must call again within three minutes, and then your phone will ring.

To be sure that the phone is on or that Do Not Disturb is on:
Go to the right-hand corner of the screen and swipe down to the left-hand corner.
Then, you'll see a picture on your screen with many options that you can choose from.

Click on Focus
At the top, you'll see Do Not Disturb
If it's glowing, it's on.
If it's not glowing, it's not active.

Open the Voice Memos app.
At the bottom right is an icon shaped like an envelope.
Click on it.
Then you will see New Folder. Give the document a name and save it.
Click on it.
Press the red button when you are ready to record.
When you want to stop the recording, press the red button again.
Now, you can listen to the recording by pressing the Start button.

You can exit this by pressing the back arrow on the top left. Then, you will see your document in the list.

You can forward the recording if you want to. The recording itself must be open, and you can see your recording in Voice Memos. Click on the recording that you want to send. Then you are in another window. Choose your recording again. You are not going to listen to it now, but there is a circle with three dots on the right side. Click on the dots. There, you can select Share and choose where you want to send the document to.

With this app, Voice Memos, you can record your own self-hypnosis to listen to later.
I recommend you send the recording to your email address because then you can open your recording on any device.

To record on Samsung Android:

Check your battery. Make sure you have enough battery to last through your recording.

Go to "Play Store."
Find "Voice Recorder."
There is a choice of several recorders.
Select "Easy Voice Recorder."
Click on it.
Press "Open."
You are now in the program.
Press "My Recording"
and clarify the document. Give it a name.
Then press "Done" at the bottom of the page.
You are now on a white page with a red button at the bottom of it,
and you will see the name of your document on the page, too.
Click on the red button (the picture of a microphone).
Sometimes you need to press "Continue."

Then press the red button and start the recording.
When you need to stop, press the red button again.
Use the red button to continue, pause, and stop recording.
At the bottom of the page, the X is where you can discard the recording.
On the other side is a V, which you press to keep the recording.

When the recording has been saved, you will see there are three dots on the document.
Press the dots and press "Share."
Here you can decide where you want to send the recording.
I recommend sending the file/recording to your email address so the recording will not be lost.

Good luck to you.

In the next chapters, the scripts are coming one after another. There are a total of nine scripts in this book, and each script has its own chapter. There are good explanations, so you can create your own script for your own self-hypnosis.

In the scripts, I think it's best to read the text as if you're talking to someone next to you. The plan is to read it into your phone and listen to your own self-hypnosis script in your own voice. That's why I always use "YOU" as if I'm talking to a person sitting next to me.

It is very individual how each of us want this to be.
But it is easy to change this and use "I" instead of "YOU" if you like that better. We are doing these scripts for ourselves, and we make them just as we think is best.

Each self-hypnosis starts with an INDUCTION, then a DEEPENING. After that, you can start working toward the goals and suggestions that you want to use for yourself in self-hypnosis.

Induction are words for how we say things at the beginning of hypnosis to induce relaxation and calmness.

There are various types of inductions and here is an overview of the most commonly used ones.

The Main Inductions

Muscle relaxation	Relax the whole body well.
Visualization	Use your imagination and see a picture in your mind.
Autogenic training	Focus on heat and weight to induce self-hypnosis.
Affirmation	Repeat positive statements to influence the subconscious.
Counting methods	Countdown to deepen the relaxation and achieve self-hypnosis.
Breathing exercises	Do certain breathing exercises to get into relaxation.
Body scan	Scan your body. Focus your attention on different parts of the body to promote relaxation.

Guided imagery	Following a pre-recorded script or memorizing the hypnosis yourself to achieve certain results.
Eye fixation	Bringing attention to a specific place or staring at a point to achieve relaxation.

All these inductions are used in the scripts in this book. You can use any inductions you want or piece them together for your own self-hypnosis.
Next comes deepening, to deepen the relaxation even more.
To find even more peace.

The Main Deepeners

Counting down	Counting backward from a higher number to a lower number, often looking at each number separately.
Stairs	Imagine going downstairs, where each step takes you deeper into relaxation.
Progressive relaxation	Systematically relaxing each part of the body from head to toe or vice versa.
Visual deepening	Create images in your mind where you feel comfortable,

	everything is energized and peaceful, and you are in your favorite place.
Breathing awareness	Focus on your breathing, count backward and imagine breathing in relaxation and calmness and breathing out all tension and stress.
Body scan	Mentally scan the body for tension and release it.
Metaphors	Use metaphors such as turning off the light or sinking into a comfortable chair or floating on a cloud.

These techniques are all also in the scripts in this book. Where do you find the scripts that match each one?

Chapter 5	:	Light Switch. Get relaxation and calm over the whole body.
Chapter 6	:	Better Sleep and more peace of mind.
Chapter 7	:	Fill the mind with beautiful light—Increase Well-Being, Energy, Health, and capacity in various areas.
Chapter 8	:	Self-Hypnosis and Golf.

Chapter 9	:	Self-Hypnosis for Pain Relief, Parts Therapy. Get rid of fear. Strengthen vision. See yourself healthy and fit.
Chapter 10	:	Feeling better in general, increasing self-confidence. Work with the various problems and addictions. Increase gratitude, optimism, and happiness. The Word, the Circle, Mindfulness, Confidence.
Chapter 11	:	Getting rid of bad feelings. The Timeline and the Cloud. Go back in time along the timeline and reset your mind. You are the only one who can change your thoughts.
Chapter 12	:	Thomas Edison's technique. This method is the simplest way to get rid of worry and anxiety and solve problems and increase happiness and well-being.
Chapter 13	:	Betty Erickson's self-hypnosis method, releasing tension and stress.
Chapter 14	:	The final chapter of this book. Summary and encouragement.

With these scripts, you can do all the self-hypnosis you want.
You can take what suits you best and put together one script from many scripts. These scripts can help many people with different desires.

When you are going into self-hypnosis, it's best to keep your attention there. Do not engage in self-hypnosis while driving or operating machinery.

Chapter 5

Self-Hypnosis to Relax Your Body and Find Inner Peace

The Light Switch Script

When you read this out and record it on your phone:

Read at your usual speed, do not rush.
Speak naturally and not too slowly.
Stop for a little while after each line.

Keep your goal in mind and the suggestions you want to work with in this self-hypnosis. Keep your suggestions positive and in the present tense. There are instructions here in the script where you can insert your own suggestions. The embedded lines are for information.

It is good to know how long you are going to give to your self-hypnosis. You can set your mind to a specific time or set a timer or clock.

And then start the recording from here:

Take a deep breath in and out...
allow yourself to relax.

Take a deep breath in again,
and when you exhale,
allow your whole body to relax.
Take another deep breath in
and when you exhale,
allow your eyes to close.

Bring your attention to your body.
If there is any tension anywhere in the body,
then notice it
and allow that part of your body to completely relax.

Move your mind over your body and let it relax.
Your head is completely relaxed,
your neck,
your shoulders are relaxed and loose.
Your upper body is completely loose and limp.
Your hands
they are as powerless as they can get.
It's a very pleasant feeling.
The lower part of your body is completely relaxed
and also, your legs
all the way down to your ankles
and all the way to the toes.
The whole body is completely calm.

Think about how your mind is connected to your body.
Visualize these connections like electrical wires
that connect the body and the mind.

That's a lot of bundles of wire
which connect certain areas.

Each bundle has a switch.
When you turn off the switch,
that part disconnects, controlled by this switch.
There are bundles of wires that connect to your muscles.
There are bundles of wires connected to your thoughts.

There is a switch associated with each part.
And you can turn these switches on or off.

You can activate the switches.
Focus your attention on any part of your body.

By focusing on one specific part of the body,
the correct switch will be selected.
There is a connection between that part of the body
and a certain part of the mind.
And there is a switch that controls that connection.

It's like turning a light switch on and off.
When you turn off the switch
then that part of the body relaxes instantly.

Think about the part of your body that you want to relax now.

Now focus on your hands.
Under each finger is a switch.
You choose which switch is appropriate for each group of wires.
When you press down a finger,
you turn that switch on or off.

Think about what part of your body you want to see right now.

Let your mind choose your fingers.
Now, lift your finger and click your finger down.
The part of your body that you are focused on relaxes.
Lift your finger again and snap it down.
and another part of the body that you choose relaxes.
You allow complete relaxation there.
The muscles become weak, and soft, and heavy.

It's like turning off the lights in an entire building.
Move your finger and turn off the switch,
and the lights go out.
Each department separately
or the whole building at once
depending on how your switches are connected....
a good metaphor for your body and mind,
which is completely relaxed, and you feel very comfortable.

Bring your suggestion here into your self-hypnosis where you connect your target to a bunch of wires...
where you can turn off this feeling.
And envision how you want your mind set.
Focus on something positive and in the present that helps you feel better.

"I turn off parts of my body by turning off the switch."
"I feel this wonderful calm when I turn off the switch."
"I get rid of stress by turning off the appropriate switch."

You are in a wonderful state of self-hypnosis.

If thoughts,
feelings,
or concerns come to mind, then it's okay.
Notice each thought,
admit it,
and activate the switch associated with this thought,
and then you turn off that thought.

And when that thought turns off,
you can relax even more deeply.

Repeat this for each thought you want to control,
and when you turn off that thought,

and you will go deeper and deeper.

Then, you can also turn on the switch
to turn on something new that you want in life.
It is possible to use the switches
to turn off something old and
to turn on something new.

Now, let your mind dwell there.
And clean your mind.
Visualize the changes you just made.

Keep your thoughts positive and focused
and in the present, where you see yourself
having achieved your goals and suggestions.
Stay there as long as you need or have time to.

> Give some time here to pause where you don't say anything in the recording,
> to allow the mind to connect and visualize the changes.

It's so comfortable to come in quietness back from self-hypnosis.

Note how you feel right now.

Summon optimism, confidence, and joy,
and visualize them always being by your side.

When you are ready to come back from self-hypnosis, then count from 1 to 5.
Come back at your own pace. Do not hurry.

1 -   2 -   3 -   4 -   5 –

Come back slowly... everything at your own pace.
And you feel wonderful.
You feel full of energy,
but still in a good state of relaxation
and with this inner peace,
which is so sweet.

And you're ready to tackle what the day has to offer.

NOTE: The above script is my own, but some of the ideas in this chapter come from https://besthypnosisscripts.com/

Chapter 6

Self-Hypnosis to Get Better Sleep and Achieve More Calm

Before you go into self-hypnosis:
Keep your goal and suggestions clearly in your mind. You can create your own script based on the script below by inserting your goal and suggestions.

You can read the self-hypnosis script into your phone and listen to it when you want to go into self-hypnosis. (See Chapter 4.)

When you record this on your phone:

- Read at your usual speed and don't rush.
- Speak naturally and understandably.
- Stop a little after each line.

This way, it is more comfortable to listen to.

Now we can start.

You can include this text in your recording if you want,
or you can start a little further down
where you go directly to self-hypnosis.

Anxiety and fear are often
what keep people up when they are trying to fall asleep,
and some have difficulty falling back asleep
when they wake up.

It's not just stress.
This is a condition or problem in life
that people often have to face.

Sometimes, this is a health condition,
a bad health diagnosis,
a general illness,
or various disturbing experiences.

Sometimes, there are problems in our personal life,
in relationships,
or financial problems,
which can be related to anxiety or fear.
So, when your head rests on the pillow,
your mind goes off with a lot of thoughts,
and you start thinking about all these challenges that scare you.
The fear is always for the future or the present moment.

Use this script whenever you need it,
especially when you are going to sleep,
to break this vicious cycle of fear.

Self-Hypnosis script for better sleep

Take a deep breath
and feel the oxygen flow to your lungs
and as you exhale,
your mind is getting rid of anything you don't need right now.
Find a spot on the wall in front of you
above eye level and stare at it.
Count from three to one.

3 2 1

Close your eyes.

Now count from one to three.

1 2 3

Open your eyes,
staring at the same spot as before.

Always stare at the same spot
when you have your eyes open.

3 2 1

Close your eyes.
Feel the relaxation come to you.
It feels so good to close your eyes.
1 2 3

Open your eyes and stare at the same point.

3 2 1

Close your eyes.
Great.
Go deeper and deeper.

1 2 3

Open your eyes.
When you feel that your eyes are struggling to open, then just say:

3 2 1

and close your eyes
and go deeper and deeper into relaxation.

Feel how pleasant it is
to get this calmness.
And allow you to go deeper into self-hypnosis.

Now, slowly count backward from 5 to 1:

5 More and more relaxed
4 It is so pleasant to feel this calm
3 You go deeper and feel better and better
2 You just listen to your voice, whether it's in your mind or you're listening to a recording, and allow yourself to enjoy the relaxation
1 You have entered a deep, wonderful relaxation, and enjoy being in this calmness

Now, in your mind,
go to a peaceful place
where you always feel good.

Let your imagination work with you
to take you there.
Maybe this is a real place,
or maybe it only exists in the mind.
A favorite place
that is really special for you to go to.
Visualize yourself in that place.
Enjoy being there.
Find a place there
where you can sit or lie down

Allow yourself to be at peace
while allowing your mind to work with you
in changing what you want to change, fix, or reset.
Right now, your subconscious mind is in charge.

You don't know
why you feel this anxiety and fear
until perhaps when you try to go to sleep.
Then the thoughts come,
and you try to find the cause,
but finding the cause
is actually not the same
as finding the solution.

Sleep reduces fear.
So, sleep and relaxation help you to feel better.
The immune system
becomes more active when we sleep,
and the fear decreases.

Sometimes, we have fear
that goes far and wide throughout the body,
and physical problems appear.

Some lights in the mind take over.
These lights need to be turned off
despite everything being off in the real world.
Then you have to "turn off the lights" in your mind.
Picture in your mind the light switch,
the switch you use to turn off the lights.
Visualize yourself raising your finger,
putting your finger on the switch,
and turning off the lights.
Click ...... with your finger.
And the darkness comes, and everything is turned off,

and you have your eyes firmly closed.

Visualize in your mind
that you are standing at a line.
The line can be similar to a line
painted on the grass on a football field.
There may also be lines elsewhere,
painted with a brush
wherever you can think of.
Maybe a yellow line along the middle of the road.

Wherever that line is,
imagine you are standing at that line.
This line represents the present, NOW,
this moment, NOW.
Everything that is on the other side of the line,
is perhaps anxiety or fear.
But you are at the line looking over it.
Look to the fear; look to the anxiety.
Whatever it is, let yourself see it for a moment.
Admit the fear just for a moment.
You are not going to connect to the fear.
You are simply a part of it,
and you tell yourself
as you stand at the line
that the fear or anxiety
or whatever you are afraid of
is on the other side of the line.

Notice that everything is on the other side of the line,
whether it is fear, anxiety,
or any other feeling.
It can't get to you,
but you can see it.
You are going to see your fear
or whatever it is
mental or physical.

Seeing the fear is often half the recovery.
Since this is on the other side of the line,
it is not coming to you.

So, imagine this
as it is on the other side of the line.
Your own mind
gives you even more calmness
despite the fear
at the present moment.

And you are completely safe.

> Here, you can enter your goal that you brought to this self-hypnosis,
> the goal you wrote down.
> Use your suggestions and repeat them several times.
> Present them in the present tense as if you have achieved your goal.

Keep all the suggestions positive and something you would like to see or experience in your life. These are some of the changes you want in your life.

Examples:

"I feel great inner peace and am free from fear and anxiety."

"Now I will sleep soundly tonight because I know how to leave my anxiety somewhere else."

"I am free from tension and worry, and I embrace calmness and love within me. "

"I am fearless and positive and surrounded by peace and comfort."

"My mind is clear and focused, and I am free from unnecessary worries."

"Sleep is now nourishing and sweet, and I sleep all night."

Use what suits you, and of course, you can also create your own suggestions.
You can see how this is done from these examples.

You can also insert this elsewhere in the script just as you see fit.

Then the script continues:

Because you see clearly
you step back
one step at a time
and away from the fear and anxiety
because it is on the other side of the line.

Going further and further away from the line,
from the fear and anxiety.

Now you can go back to bed
in your mind or in reality
and allow sleep to come to you.
You will notice that simply by being in the present
knowing that the anxiety or fear
is on the other side of the line
then you feel relief.

Feel that you can go into a pleasant, nourishing sleep
and sleep sweetly until the new morning.
There is a line between you and fear or anxiety
and you have come a long way from this.

Maybe not all fear goes away right away.
But maybe it will leave immediately
and at least enough so that you can close your eyes

and allow these feelings
to leave you
So, you get your necessary rest.

Allow yourself to find the stillness within
and allow yourself to fall asleep
as pleasant a sleep as possible.

Here you have two possibilities:
Go to sleep or wake up

If you want to go to sleep:

Allow yourself to go to sleep in peace and quiet.
Allow yourself to enjoy the sleep
and wake up in the morning
refreshed and full of energy.
The recording stops
and does not disturb you in any way
and you drift off into a peaceful sleep.

Or:

Then it's time to come back from hypnosis

Count from 1 to 5 slowly

1 2 3 4 5

Open your eyes
You are refreshed and feel wonderful.

NOTE: This script is based on the method by Dr. Richard K. Nongard.

Dr. Richard K. Nongard is a world-renowned keynote speaker. He has written over thirty books in his career on counseling, psychology, professional hypnosis, and leadership. His newest book is "Confidence in Hypnotherapy Practice:
An interpretive Phenomenological analysis" July 2024

He has two Ph.D. One in psychology from California Southern University and another in Transformational Leadership from Bakke Graduate University which he completed in July 2024.

Chapter 7

Increase Well-Being, Health, and Energy

You can record this hypnosis script on your phone to listen to later if you wish. Instructions for that are in this book.

You can also memorize this script and go into this self-hypnosis in your mind.

This hypnosis is to fill the mind with beautiful light and thus achieve the change you desire,
such as improving capacity in various areas and increasing well-being, better health, more energy, getting rid of pain, getting a calm mind, increasing self-confidence, and so on.

Find a good place where you will not be disturbed during the self-hypnosis. Turn off your phone, computer, and anything that could disturb you at this moment.

Do not listen to your self-hypnosis recording while operating machinery.

Script to Increase Well-Being, Health, and Energy:

Let yourself go into deep relaxation
and enjoy feeling great calmness.
Allow calmness and ease to come to you,
and let yourself enjoy it.

Pay attention to your breathing.
Take a deep breath
and try to relax as much as possible.
Then exhale and let go of whatever is bothering you.
Let it to go with your exhalation.

With every breath
let yourself go deeper and deeper.
This is a good way for the body
to feel at ease,
and to find inner peace,
deliberation,
and calmness.

Each breath takes you deeper and deeper into relaxation.
Allow the muscles in your entire body to completely relax.
Bring attention to your eyes.

Let your eyes find complete peace
and calm down all the small muscles around your eyes.

It's so nice to feel the relaxation in your eyes.
When you have managed to relax your eyes,
then the whole face is calm.

Your forehead is completely slack,
the cheeks and the chin ......
and the lower jaw are completely slack.

Feel that your neck is completely relaxed
and all the muscles in your back, too.
Hands completely relaxed
chest cavity.........
abdomen,
All your organs in complete relaxation.
Yet your organs are
to perform their duty as expected of them.

Complete relaxation in the whole body.

Feel that your legs are completely relaxed
right down to the toes.
Allow yourself to go deeper and deeper into relaxation,
just as deep as you wish.
You are always in charge.

When the body is in this pleasant deep state,
imagine ...... or visualize

a beautiful ball of light
is coming to your vortex and
sits on top of your head.
And this light spreads throughout your body,
through the vortex.
A beautiful and powerful light.
This light is connected to what is around you.

This is a healing light to fix and improve what is needed.
This light wants to heal every cell
and heals every organ of the body.
It relieves you of discomfort.......... if there is any.

The light fills all cells and tissues with healing light
the face
the head
the neck.
Soothes and relaxes all the muscles in the neck
hands,
the spinal cord,
the heart,
and spreads your beautiful energy,
which is stored in the heart.

Heals your heart and lungs
and the light shines so beautifully
and you go deeper and deeper.

Find what makes you feel good and what makes you feel at peace.

You go deeper and deeper with each breath.

The light continues down into the abdomen
Heals, repairs, and resets the energy there.
Goes to the hips
and down both legs
with great relaxation and calmness.
The legs are so relaxed, and everything is so still,
and you go even deeper.

You can listen to your voice,
but all other sounds in the environment are irrelevant to you.
They don't bother you at all.
You don't care about them.

These external sounds
simply help you go even deeper into relaxation.

Visualize or imagine now
that the light surrounds your whole body also externally.
Just as if you were inside a ball of light.
And this light protects you.
It's just positivity, kindness, and optimism
which comes with this light,
All the positive things you can think of
follow the light.

You are now in deep hypnosis,
in great calmness, and you feel very good.

Here, you can bring in the suggestions, the goals, you wrote for yourself.
You can open your eyes and read the suggestions from the paper, or you may have your suggestions in your mind, or you may have recorded them already. Remember to keep all your suggestions positive and in the present tense.
Talk to yourself as if you have already achieved your goal.

"I'm doing so well in golf. My strokes are long and straight."

"I'm so relaxed and fully focused on what I'm doing."

"I quit smoking, and I'm so proud of myself."

"I exercise regularly and walk every day."

"I'm so happy with myself and full of energy."

Repeat the suggestions several times.
Visualize in your mind what you are calling to you.
Use your imagination.

When you are ready to come back from self-hypnosis:

Pause for a moment
and allow your mind to receive all your suggestions.

Visualize yourself vividly
where you have achieved your goals
and you feel so good.
You are so proud of yourself
and look forward with bright eyes.
Now, fill up your energy and well-being.
Feel the energy flowing to you
where you need it the most.

Take a moment for this.

When you are ready to come back from self-hypnosis,
then count from 1–5
Come back in peace
at your own pace.

1 2 3 4 5
wide awake,
and refreshed, and full of energy.
Totally ready to tackle the day's tasks with a smile on your face.

And it feels wonderful.

Chapter 8

Self-Hypnosis for Golfers

Many people let emotions like anxiety or anger get in the way of the concentration needed to achieve a good golf swing.

Self-hypnosis can be of great help to golfers who want to improve their focus, reduce anxiety, and increase their golf performance.

For self-hypnosis to help, you need to use your imagination.
See in your mind's eye you are playing very well.
You must be relaxed for it to go well.
Away with all the stress.
Have a single focus on what you are doing.
It's good to practice breathing and general relaxation as well as playing golf.
Be positive and calm.

Believe that you can do this: "I trust my swing."
Practice in your mind that you are playing an entire round of golf.

Here comes a script to improve your golf score. Focus your mind on relaxation,
visualize yourself playing golf and feel the joy that follows.

Feel free to record this script on your smartphone and play it over and over again.
You can edit and add to the script as you want.

Find a comfortable place
where you will not be disturbed for 10–15 minutes.
It's good to sit in a chair or lie down.
Do not cross your legs or arms.

Self-Hypnosis script for golf:

Take a deep breath in,
and as you exhale, close your eyes
and feel the eyelids get heavy over your eyes.
It feels so good to close your eyes.

Feel the relaxation spread throughout the body.
Use your imagination
and visualize in your mind
what I'm about to tell you.

The Solar Plexus is a chakra in the body,
one of the seven chakras.
It is located just below the sternum
a collection of nerves located from the abdomen.

This chakra is known as the power centre.
This chakra governs our ability to be confident, decisive, and make decisions, based on our inner wisdom.
When the chakra is balanced, then we are optimistic,
we have good self-confidence,
are proactive,
and feel good.

It is also the key to unlocking our personal power
and building a strong sense of self.

Visualize there are connections from this chakra
to your hands and feet, shoulders and heart.
Visualize the connection in your mind with each sentence.

"My right arm is heavy and warm."
"My right arm is heavy and warm."
"My right arm is heavy and warm."
"My left arm is heavy and warm."
"My left arm is heavy and warm."
"My left arm is heavy and warm."
"Both my arms are heavy and warm."
"Both my arms are heavy and warm."
"Both my arms are heavy and warm."

"My neck and shoulders are heavy."
"My neck and shoulders are heavy."
"My neck and shoulders are heavy."
"My heartbeat is calm and regular."
"My heartbeat is calm and regular."
"My heartbeat is calm and regular."
"My left leg is heavy and warm."
"My left leg is heavy and warm."
"My left leg is heavy and warm."
"My right leg is heavy and warm."
"My right leg is heavy and warm."
"My right leg is heavy and warm."
"Both my legs are heavy and warm."
"Both my legs are heavy and warm."
"Both my legs are heavy and warm."
"My solar plexus is warm and comfortable."
"My solar plexus is warm and comfortable."
"My solar plexus is warm and comfortable."
"My forehead is cool."
"My forehead is cool."
"My forehead is cool."
"I feel very good."
"I feel very good."
"I feel very good."

Great!

Allow yourself to count down from 5 to 1
and with each count, you go deeper and deeper into relaxation.

5 Feels wonderful
4 Travel deeper and deeper
3 Feel better and better
2 A great calm has come over you
1 Complete relaxation and great calm

Still awake but in a very good state of relaxation.
You want to use this self-hypnosis
to improve focus,
reduce anxiety,
and improve your golf performance.
It is so much fun to play golf,
and even more fun when it goes well.
It has everything to do with the mind.

Picture yourself standing on the golf course
and about to play a round of golf.
Feel the grass under your feet
and feel the breeze on your skin.
Listen to the birds singing around you.
Feel the stillness in your mind.
You are in a very good state of relaxation
and now your subconscious is ready
to work with you in what you want to work with.

> Here, you can enter your goals that you intend to use in this self-hypnosis to improve your well-being and self-confidence in golf and do better in the area you want to improve.

You can use any of these suggestions for your own self-hypnosis if you like or create your own. You can have one suggestion or more. You can see by these examples how to make the suggestions.

Examples:

"I am calm and focused on the pitch."
"I can play golf well."
"Every hit gives me joy and confidence."
"I play my best golf effortlessly."
"I'm doing my best, and I'm competing with myself."
"I'm so happy when I'm playing golf."

You are now in deep relaxation,
and with that comes increased concentration.
Now, your mind is open to positive suggestions
that will improve your golf game.
Picture yourself at the first tee.
You are always in control in your life
and in everything you do.
You hold the driver and are starting the game.
You line up and are ready to start.
You look at the ball that is on the tee.
You have taken the direction you want the ball to go.
You take the backswing and feel the club swing perfectly
and you swing through and hit the ball very well.
See the ball soar down the fairway far and straight.

See yourself in your mind.

Now, you walk to the ball where it is on the fairway.
Hit the next shot and use your mind and imagination.
You have the direction and distance in mind.
Hit the ball lightly, and it goes straight
into the green.
Great!
Walk up to the green. Find how good it feels.
Then all that's left is to putt.
You line up on the green to putt.
You can clearly see the line to the hole in your mind.
You feel absolute concentration.
Hit lightly and safely
and the ball rolls exactly as you envisioned.

> You can repeat this text when you make your own hypnosis script or just stop here and come back from self-hypnosis.

Find how happy you are and feel comfortable.
Feel how great it is to be able to talk to yourself in your mind
and be able to use suggestions
to change what you want to change.

The mind is always ready to work with you
if the suggestions are clear
and the mind understands what you want.

Then, it's time to come back from self-hypnosis
and you do that by counting from 1–5.
Come out of the relaxation in peace.
You are not in a hurry.

1 Come back calm and quiet.
2 Begin to hear the sounds around you.
3 Move your finger and toes.
4 Take a deep breath in.
5 You can open your eyes when you are ready.

You will come back from self-hypnosis refreshed and full of energy.

"The perfect golf swing will get you 'in gear.'
Hypnosis for golf is so effective because it stops the mental chatter that creates tension that ultimately destroys your swing."

Richard K. Nongard

Chapter 9

Self-Hypnosis and Pain

Pain is the body's way of telling us that something is wrong and that we need to pay attention to it and do something to get rid of the pain.

A doctor should always be consulted in the beginning when it is appropriate. Before using hypnosis to get rid of pain, you must be sure that the pain is of a nature that does not require medical help.

We need to pay attention to it if the body brings pain to us. Why are we being sent this message? What is wrong with the body? What can we do about it?

The subconscious mind keeps track of all that is happening involuntarily in the body. It is giving us these messages for some reason. The subconscious triggers the pain in order for us to react.

For us to be able to talk about something specific in our mind, such as a pain, we need to be able to visualize it in a picture in our mind or in a perception that is normal to us. We say that in the mind, there are many elements, and each element controls its function.

Heartbeat, joy, optimism, helpfulness, and pain—and, of course, countless other things—are elements that are inside us.

When we put it in our mind like this, it is easier to visualize it when we are working on a solution.

There is an element of the subconscious that keeps track and sends us messages about pain in a certain place in our bodies.

In self-hypnosis, we talk to this specific aspect.

Let's get them to change the message because it no longer serves any purpose. Maybe they served a purpose at some point, but not anymore. There is no reason for these pains. They just are.
Maybe we know why there is pain, and we cannot do anything about it. Then it's good to be able to talk to our mind and get it to reduce the messages about pain or simply get rid of these messages that don't help anyone.

It's so interesting about the mind that we choose how we react to our thoughts.

The mind is so powerful and always wants us to feel the best.
The mind is, of course, ourself, and we want us to be healthy and feel good in all situations.
We need to be clear in our minds how we want to feel and what life is like when we are pain-free.
Then, you can use those suggestions in self-hypnosis when you talk to your mind for change.

"I would like to ask the subconscious mind to see this aspect of the mind, and talk to it, and negotiate with it to change the message ......"

Make suggestions that are suitable.
Keep them positive, in the present tense, and figurative.

"My body is a haven of comfort and tranquility."
"I float in euphoria, and my body feels wonderful."
"My mind and body are in perfect balance."
"Every moment brings me comfort and relief."
"I embrace the pleasant feeling that is all around me."
"I feel a great warmth that gives me peace and well-being."

Examples of suggestions to get rid of leg pain:

"My legs feel more relaxed and comfortable with every breath."

"Soothing warmth flows through my legs and dissolves all discomfort."

"I envision a healing light surrounding my feet and reducing all tension."

"I send a wave of relaxation from my hips down to my toes."

These suggestions can also be used for other types of pain; just change the wording so that it fits the pain you are dealing with.

When you read the script, allow a little time after each sentence so that the mind receives each suggestion well.

Self-Hypnosis script for pain

Make yourself comfortable and let yourself feel well
where you will not be interrupted for 10–15 minutes.
Allow yourself to relax as much as you can.
Allow your head to be supported by the back of the chair or sofa.
Do not cross your arms or legs.
Look at a specific point on the wall.
Now you are going to count down from 100
and when you count even numbers, your eyes are closed.
When you count in odd numbers, you open your eyes.

100 eyes simply closed,

take a deep breath and relax

99 eyes open, pull back in and relax well

98 close your eyes and imagine that you let go of all the worries of the day

as easily as you exhale

97 open your eyes

you find it getting harder and harder to open your eyes

96 eyes closed good

Find yourself wanting to go deeper and deeper

95 Easy to forget

94 Difficult to remember whether they should be open or closed

and as soon as you forget, they are closed

and you just relax deeper and deeper

93 Good

92 Deeper and deeper

So open to react to the voice

91 Go deeper and deeper

90 Your eyes just want to be closed

Forgetting to remember or remembering to forget.

Open or closed, closed or open.

You notice that the mind can think many times faster

than the spoken word

so, your conscious mind is free to listen or wander

or do both ....

while your subconscious is free

to hear and respond to your voice

start talking a little faster)

88–86 deeper and deeper. Easy to forget.

84–82 Hard to tell, whether they should be open or closed

79–74 the numbers go away so quickly now

that you feel that you just want to go deeper

and your eyes just want to be closed.

73 Every time you forget to remember or remember to forget

open or closed, odd or even,

then you just go deeper and deeper and deeper and deeper.

60–50	Eyes closed, and you go deeper,
40	forget to remember. Remember to forget.
30	Feels good

Now you are in a very relaxing state of self-hypnosis.
See in your mind's eye
where you are walking around
in a beautiful place where you feel as good as possible.
Then visualize a beautiful staircase.
You are drawn to this staircase
which fits so well into the environment.

There are ten steps on this staircase
and it leads you to your peaceful place
which is such a pleasant place
where you always feel so comfortable.
Where you can be in peace and quiet
and enjoy being in wonderful relaxation.

Now, you go to the staircase,
and you want to go down this staircase,
and go to your peaceful place
which is right below.
You are standing at the top of 10 steps and you set off...

9th step	and going deeper and deeper
8th step	feel better and better as you go deeper and deeper
7th step	Deeper and deeper
6th step	It is so sweet to feel the relaxation come to you.
5th step	Halfway down the stairs.
	Look at your peaceful place, which is so beautiful.
4th step	the deeper you go, the better you feel.
3rd step	the better you feel, the deeper you go into relaxation.
2nd step	See into your peaceful place.
	It is so beautiful and very calm.
1st step	Just one more step to your wonderful peaceful place.

And now you step into your peaceful place—your haven.
There is only positivity and optimism.
Nothing else can get in there.
It's so good to have such a place in your mind
that you can go to when needed
and get relaxation and energy,
to continue your daily life.
It's good to have a little break from everyday life

where you can refill your energy.

Find a place in your peaceful place
where you can sit or lie down
where you feel fine, as fine as possible
and you are to start working in your mind
to get rid of the pains that are bothering you.
The subconscious mind is working with you there
toward the changes you want to get.

In the mind, there are many parts
and each part holds its own role.

It is one aspect of your mind
which manages to ignite this feeling—
that certain feeling that gives you pain
in this particular place.

A feeling that is unnecessary as far as you know.
You need to have help to get rid of this pain.
It is a thought that brings an image to mind
and you are reacting to the thought.
It's all about how we talk to ourselves in our minds.
You can make positive suggestions about
how you want to feel in a certain situation.
The suggestion need not be true.
The mind reacts even though the suggestion is not true.
Just make a suggestion
that is positive, in the present tense,

worded in a good way and creates a good picture in the mind.
That's just the way it is.

Imagination is what helps us the most.
Let your imagination run wild
to get the clearest picture or experience in mind
then the subconscious understands best and reacts.

Bring your attention to what you want to work with in this self-hypnosis.

On a scale of 0–10, where is the pain?
Where is the pain located?
How is the shape of it?
What color is it?
Can you move it?
Try.
Move the pain to the right and to the left,
rotating the pain so that it spins in circles
faster and faster and faster
and let it whisk away from you
far away from you.

Go back into your mind and check where the pain is on the scale now.
Has it shrunk?

Where is the pain located now?
How is the shape of it now?

What color is it now?
Can you move it?
Try.
Move the pain to the right and to the left,
rotating the pain so that it spins in circles
Turn it so that it spins in circles
faster and faster and faster
and let it whisk away from you
far away from you.
See this happening in your mind.
Where on the scale is the pain now?
The pain that was
changes shape and color and dissolves.

> This can be repeated again and again
> until the pain is gone or the pain is much less.

You see yourself as a winner
you have no pain or discomfort
and you feel better and better.
You will feel that your health will always get better and better,
and you can do the various things that you want to do.

Visualize yourself walking through a peaceful place
where you are completely pain-free and feel wonderful.

> Here you can come up with your suggestions to be pain-free.
> Have the suggestions positive,

in the present tense,
and the picture in your mind or the sense of it very clear.

There are many suggestions
at the beginning of the chapter
that you can choose from and incorporate here into your own self-hypnosis,
and here are a few more:

"I'm in control of how I feel, and I think it's wonderful."

"I breathe in well-being and breathe out what is troubling me."

"I'm in a good place where I feel good, and my body is pain-free and feels wonderful."

And on with the script:

Take a moment now
as you get time to allow your subconscious mind
to work on those projects,
you've been wishing for.
Get everything the way it should be:
pain-free and feeling good.

Then it's time to come back from your self-hypnosis You can do it by counting from 1 to 5.

1. You will be aware of the place and time.
2. You will hear more of the external sounds around you.
3. Move your fingers and toes and wake up.
4. Take a deep breath and bring oxygen into every cell of your body.
5. You can open your eyes when you are ready.Comes back full of energy, feeling wonderful, completely pain-free.

Chapter 10

Using Self-Hypnosis to Feel Better

Self-hypnosis is a very good way to change something in your life, or allow you to feel better in many areas of life.

Write down on a piece of paper what you want to reach for yourself in this self-hypnosis.

It could be:

Joy, contentment, confidence, serenity, happiness, optimism, gratitude, respect, anticipation, consideration, stopping smoking, etc.

Write one word on the piece of paper.
This WORD describes what is important to you
to change or get into your life.
Focus on the WORD you wrote
and hold the paper in your hand
where you can watch it

and envision it,
even though your eyes are closed.

Before we begin,
find a comfortable chair to sit in
or lie down
where you feel good.

And then we begin

Taking care of yourself,
find a good position
in your chair or on your bed
so, you feel good.

Take a deep breath,
and when you exhale,
close your eyes.

Place your hands where you feel comfortable.
Pay attention to your body
and the relaxation that takes place.
Let all the muscles of the body relax.

Put yesterday's worries
and anxiety or fear for tomorrow aside,
and be totally aware
of today.
External sounds
don't matter to you.

They don't bother you at all,
and you don't care about them.
The only thing they do for you
is that they bring you even deeper into relaxation.

Yet you are always awake,
and it is you
who controls the journey
in this relaxation.
Notice that your eyes are very relaxed,
and all the muscles around the eyes are
quite weak.

The eyelids are heavy over the eyes,
and you like to keep your eyes closed.
Your cheeks are relaxed.
Your lower jaw is completely relaxed.
Feel how good it is
to achieve this calm.

Allow your shoulders to sag,
and relax well.
The whole body is completely relaxed.

This is going great.

You are not sleeping
but you are in a good, deep, relaxation.

To go even deeper into relaxation,

count backward from 5 to 1.

At each number,
simply double
this wonderful relaxation,
and allow yourself to enter this state of mind,
relaxation, and well-being
that manages
how you solve the various issues,
how you go about learning new things,
and being confident.

5 4

With every count and every breath,
you double the relaxation,
And as you get deeper into relaxation,
you feel better and better,
and the subconscious takes over.
But the subconscious can change everything
that you want to change.

3 2

The heartbeat is already calmer and slower
and your breathing is sweet and rhythmic.

1

Your attention is sharp now,

because
what you have done
in a few minutes,
is changing your mind
and finding solutions,
and getting your subconscious to work with you.

You followed the suggestions
to create this wonderful experience.

When you breathe in,
you feel how the oxygen
goes very deep into the lungs.
You feel how the oxygen flows into your body
and into your bloodstream.
And when you exhale,
you exhale all the stress and things that are bothering you,
and there will be even more peace and quiet over you.

Your attention is now on the WORD
that you wrote on the paper earlier
and which you hold now in your palm.
You picture it in your mind.
Your mind perceives this WORD.
you can see how important it is to you
to achieve this goal
to which the word refers.
Visualize yourself
where you have already

achieved your goal.
Feel how you feel.
Find how happy you are.

Look at the WORD
Maybe it's clearly written, or maybe not,
perhaps as if the word is merging with the paper.
Despite having your eyes closed,
you will see the WORD before you.

You have set aside this time
for self-hypnosis
to learn how to create a solution.

Experience this WORD.

You can say the WORD in your mind
and repeat it
because it gives power to the WORD.

Be happy with yourself
for a great job you are working on now.
Not just by
paying attention
to your written WORD,
but by allowing yourself
mentally and physically
to unite with this word,
and bring it to this process,
and feel at ease.

Allow your attention now
to return to your breathing.

Find a place in your mind
which is peaceful and where you feel good.
Some quiet place in your mind.
It can be a place that you have established before
and you feel comfortable in.
There are situations in life
where you need confidence.

Draw in your mind a CIRCLE on the floor in front of you.
This CIRCLE you are drawing on the floor
is a CIRCLE that you can step into.
And when you step into the CIRCLE
in your mind
and take a deep breath,
you feel your confidence increasing,
and stillness comes over you.
This is a silence you created
a while ago
but there's still a lot of energy.

Because whenever you take a deep breath,
then your mind reacts
by calling the relaxation to you,
and as you soar
or float in your mind,
you calmly allow yourself
to experience this feeling.

You are happy with who you are
and you are where you want to be,
full of confidence.
This is a place of peace.
Allow yourself to be in this place in your mind
and feel the confidence.
Visualize the WORD again
where you are full of confidence and poise,
still energetic,
and feeling very good
and can do anything you want.

You are happy with who you are
and you are at the place you want to be
full of confidence.
This is a place of peace.
Allow yourself to be in this place in your mind
and feel the confidence.

Visualize the WORD again
where you are full of confidence and poise,
still energetic
and feeling very good
and can do whatever you want to.

And it is you who creates this feeling.

A new chapter in your life is about to begin
with new behavior
where you feel confidence and acceptance

because this is a normal situation.

The mind can create this magical vision.

This RING of confidence
that you put on the floor earlier with your imagination
evokes a good feeling and well-being.
And with each inhalation,
more and more strength and success are brought to you.
Whenever you experience yourself
in this situation,
where you need to have a lot of confidence,
imagine that you draw a circle on the floor in front of you
which you can step into.
This is your circle of confidence.

Allow your attention now
to go to the WORD.
The word you choose.
Visualize it.
See yourself achieving this goal.

The circle of confidence,
that you can use whenever you want.
For meetings,
before you have to stand in front of people and speak,
and anywhere in life when it suits you.

You simply draw a CIRCLE on the floor in front of you,

you see yourself in your mind
stepping into the CIRCLE,
this imaginary CIRCLE,
and feel the confidence
grow stronger within you.

While watching the CIRCLE in your mind,
visualize
where your attention is now.

Being present is paying close attention.
Take responsibility for your experiences
and ideas.
Mindfulness is the art of living in the present,
at this moment.
Do not miss the past
or be afraid of the future.
It is at this moment
that we are whole and complete.

Mindfulness teaches us to experience life and
experience our thoughts and feelings
from a completely new perspective.

If you ever feel fear or dread
or other unpleasant sensations
then let your attention go to your breathing
and be in the present
to take your mind off
what is happening

and causing discomfort.
Thus, bring your mind
back to the normal state.
We can focus our mind on the breath
then the mind is there
and not on the thoughts
which perhaps are disturbing us.
This is how we can influence the mind
and focus our attention on our breathing.

You don't need to speed up
or slow down your breathing,
just feel it
when you inhale
and when you exhale.
And if it comes to your
thoughts or feelings,
then there is no need to try to stop them,
instead, look at what comes to mind
and define it.
Do not follow these thoughts,
just know about them,
and allow them to pass.
The attention is on the breathing.
If you have any sensations,
if your body feels something,
then you can simply realize
this is what the body does,
it perceives
and it experiences.

And use this as a key
to move your mind
back to the breathing.

We have covered many things in this self-hypnosis.

You wrote one WORD on a piece of paper
and held onto it.
Something you want
to be able to do or get into your life.
You are going to perceive this WORD
and allow it to influence you.
Then there was the CIRCLE,
The CIRCLE of confidence and well-being.
You draw a circle on the floor in your mind,
And step into the ring,
when you need more confidence and well-being.

Then mindfulness.
Keep your mind on
what is happening here and now.

Find calm and composure,
getting you out of situations that are causing stress and discomfort,
by bringing attention to the breathing.
With each inhalation,
you feel energy and relaxation coming to you.
And with each exhalation,
you get rid of what you no longer need...

Visualize yourself
where you have already
achieve your goal.
Feel how you feel.
Find how happy you are.

Then, it's time to come back from this pleasant relaxation, self-hypnosis.

You do that by counting from 1 to 5,
and allow yourself to come back in peace.

1 2 3

Feel that you are ready
to come back from this wonderful self-hypnosis

4 Take a deep breath and allow the oxygen to flow into every cell.

5 You can open your eyes when you are ready.

Come back refreshed and full of energy,
ready to tackle whatever the day has to offer.

N.B. Do not listen to self-hypnosis recordings while operating machinery.

Chapter 11

The Timeline and the Cloud

Get rid of old feelings that are causing problems.
Go back in time and fix or improve.

It is important to remember that while self-hypnosis can be powerful, it is not a substitute for professional therapy, especially when dealing with trauma or serious emotional issues.

If you experience very intense emotions or memories, do not hesitate to seek help from an appropriate doctor or therapist.

But when we must deal with common problems, it is good to know this method and to be aware of how powerful we are at helping ourselves.

The body knows how to heal itself, and we need to give the body and mind a chance to do so.

The Timeline and the Cloud Self-Hypnosis Method

In this self-hypnosis, the focus is on changing something in your mind that has been bothering you for years, perhaps from childhood or sometime in the past.
It is something that causes you difficult thoughts or memories that you would like to get rid of so you can carry on with your life. You really want some changes.

This method can also be used when we want to go back in time to find something we have lost and are looking for. It can be objects, knowledge, or the ability to do something.

Imagine
that you see in front of you
a timeline which is from birth to the present day.
Some see this as a road or a train track.
Others see it as a river or a mental image of a timeline
with your years, months, and days of life.

Have the problem clearly in mind
and visualize it
an incident or problem
you plan to fix or change.
This could be one particular thing
a memory

or a general feeling of well-being
at a certain period in your life.
Visualize yourself floating above the timeline.
Go back in time to this particular incident.

When you come to the incident, allow yourself to view it from a distance
or relive it.
Notice the details, your feelings, and your perception toward this.

Then, see that you change the incident in your mind so that you react in a positive way, and you feel good. Something positive.

You can also visualize yourself, where you are comforting yourself at this particular time.

Everything is done to make you feel better and get rid of what causes you unrest or discomfort.

There is no need to feel bad about something that is long gone and has nothing to do with you today.

Think about what lessons and life insights you gained from this experience.

Then, come back to the current time.
Allow a moment to process what you experienced

and then use the normal means of coming back out of self-hypnosis.

Eyelid Heaviness Script

Sit or lie down in a comfortable and quiet place
where you will not be disturbed.

Take a deep breath to relax.
Open your eyes
and focus on a place or pointe
just above eye level.

Say to yourself
"In a moment, I will close my eyes.
When I do,
I will feel a wave of relaxation come over me."

Close your eyes and take a deep breath.
Feel the relaxation come to you

Open your eyes again and say:
"Every time I close my eyes, I will go twice as deep into relaxation."

Close your eyes again,
find yourself relaxing even more deeply.

Open your eyes again and say:
"My eyelids feel heavier with each breath.

The next time I close them, they will be so heavy
and I will be so relaxed."

Close your eyes,
notice the heaviness of the eyelids and the relaxation

Open your eyes and say:
"Every time I close my eyes, I will go twice as deep into relaxation."

Close your eyes
and feel how pleasant it is to bring relaxation to it.

Open your eyes and say:
"My eyelids grow heavier with each breath.
The next time I close them, they will be so heavy
and I will feel so relaxed."

Close your eyes,
you are wonderfully relaxed
and feel wonderful.

Open your eyes, and say:
"Every time I close my eyes,
I go deeper and deeper
and always feel better and better."

Close your eyes, and say:
"My eyes are now so relaxed,
and my eyelids are heavy

and they just want to be closed,
and the relaxation allows me to go
deep into a peaceful state of relaxation."

Scan your body in your mind
from head to toe,
and release all tension
if it exists there
and allow yourself to go even deeper into relaxation.

You are not asleep—just in a pleasant state
of calm and well-being.
Now that your eyes are closed
and you have reached this pleasant relaxation
then count backward from 10 down to 1.
Visualize yourself
going deeper and deeper into relaxation
at every number you count.

10, 9, 8, 7, 6, 5, 4, 3, 2, 1.

Complete relaxation and well-being.

Find a good place to relax.
It can be out in your garden
or somewhere out in nature.
Down by the sea, in the woods
or wherever you like to be.

If you choose outdoors,
imagine
that you bring a blanket
with you, which you lay on the ground.
Then lay on the blanket
and enjoy looking up at the sky.
Allow yourself to listen
to the birds
and the flies.
Hear from the people who are far away.
You are alone where you are
and are allowing yourself to be in total relaxation.
Just relaxing and letting your mind wander.
You have decided what it is
that you are going to work on in this self-hypnosis.
Something from the past
which has been bothering you,
or something you want to remember better or find.

Visualize a timeline that runs from you
all the way to your birth.
This timeline is divided into
years, and months, and days,
and then the time of day.
You're going to look at this timeline
and fix something that's been bothering you.
There is no need to experience things
again, and again
and feel bad about them.
You choose your thoughts

and can fix and disconnect emotions
related to certain incidents.
You remember the incident from the past
and make the decision to disconnect it
so that it stops bringing discomfort.
And you do it
by allowing you
to take a closer look at your timeline.

See yourself first
where you lie on the blanket
out in nature
taking good care of yourself.
You look up at the sky
and see that it is clear blue
and there is not a cloud.
You feel the sun and its warmth on your skin
and you smell the scrub and vegetation around you.
You hear a stream running right by you.
Now you see that there is one cloud forming in the sky
and it approaches you.
You look at the cloud and it comes closer and closer.
Now it's above you,
and it trickles down to you.
You feel like you are being invited
to come and sit in the cloud.
You get up and walk to the cloud
and sit in the cloud
and you feel that
you are completely safe there.

Now the cloud rises
and ascends into the air,
not far
but high enough
so, you can see clearly down to the ground
and your timeline.
The cloud goes back in time with you
to this particular incident
which has been bothering you for a long time.
You set a goal
positive and in the present tense
where you want to get rid of that bad feeling
toward this particular incident
Now you bring your subconscious mind with you.
It is always willing to work with you,
and fix and edit and reset
if it gets a clear message and knows what to do.

You are now directly above your incident on the timeline.
You view the incident and can view it backward and forward at will.
You are determined to get rid of this bad feeling
toward this incident.

The subconscious mind is ready to work with you
and rid you of these bad feelings
and disconnect them from this incident.

You ask your unconscious mind to
disconnect this feeling,

to counter this incident.
It reacts quickly and resets these feelings.
You created a suggestion earlier,
how you want to feel
under these circumstances.
Say your suggestion now
several times in your mind.

> For example:
> "I'm free of that old feeling that was bothering me."

You see
where this change takes place.
You look at the timeline
and you see this happening.
By allowing yourself to fix this feeling
then you're feeling will be much better.
There is no need to think again and again
about something that has passed long time ago.
It is better to change the feeling toward the incident.

Disconnect that feeling now from your memory.

You remember exactly how everything was,
but you feel better
when you are done
to disconnect the feeling from the incident.

When you feel that you have fixed this feeling,

then the cloud rises again
and heads back
to the point where it reached you
at the beginning of the journey
and returns you to your blanket.

You go and lay back on the blanket
and allow your mind to wander back
to the incident
and find out how much has changed in this short time.
This is not causing problems anymore.

You are the one who controls your thoughts,
no one else can do that.
You are the one who can change
how you feel,
toward things that you are thinking.

It's so nice to know
that we can change what we think
and in return,
we get a better feeling and a happier life.
Now is the time to stand up
in your beautiful place in nature,
and gather the blanket
and go home
and come back from this self-hypnosis calmly.

Say your suggestions over and over in your mind
and feel how happy you are

for doing this great job
in your own mind.

To come back from this self-hypnosis, you are going to count from 1 to 5.

1 Coming back slowly.
2 Becoming aware of place and time.
3 It's good to move the fingers and toes.
4 Take a deep breath and feel the oxygen flow to you.
5 You can open your eyes when you are ready,

Come back from self-hypnosis refreshed and full of energy and feeling wonderful.

Chapter 12

Thomas Edison's Technique

Thomas Edison was an American inventor who was celebrated in the 19th century for his many inventions. He improved the light bulb and the telephone and invented sound recording and cinematography.

He was responsible for the electric lighting on Pearl Street in Manhattan on September 4, 1882, and for providing electricity to homes at a price comparable to gas.

This method is attributed to Thomas Edison because he used it himself when he was working and needed to increase his creativity or solve a problem.

This is a great way to increase your creativity or solve a problem.
Give yourself about an hour.

You do not need a script for this exercise.
It is very simple and easy to learn.

Before you start this exercise,
have a goal in mind.
What do you want to get out of this exercise?
Get rid of fear or anxiety?
Get better at something?
Or just bring questions to mind
and get answers?

Have paper and a pen handy.
Do not use a computer or your phone.
As soon as you wake up from the relaxation,
write your thoughts on the paper
or the answers to the questions you had in mind.
The mind is so open to ideas at this point.

The Script.

Sit down somewhere you will not be disturbed.
It does not have to be completely silent,
only that you can be left alone.
You can go into self-hypnosis by the sea
or somewhere else in nature
or just sitting in your chair at home.

There just needs to be a floor or substrate
which can be heard if something falls on the floor.

Put something in the palm of your hand
that can be heard when it falls on the floor.
Holding the object firmly, close your palm.

Edison had a small steel ball,
but you can use anything.
your keys or anything that can be heard when it falls on the floor.

Now, take care of yourself.
Some sit in the lotus position on the beach,
but just sit where you feel good,
and you won't fall asleep.

Allow yourself to relax and sink into the chair.
When you are almost asleep,
then you are relaxing your palm
and what you are holding
falls to the floor.
there needs to be a surface that
can be heard if something falls on the floor

Then you hear the sound
and wake up from the relaxation.
At this point, you have a very open mind.
The mind is very creative
and ready to come up with answers.
Think about your suggestion
or what you are going to work on in this exercise.
Say it in your mind over and over again.

Listen for an answer in your mind
and write it down on your paper.

You can also simply have
nothing in mind for this exercise
and see what comes to you.
Write down immediately what comes to mind
because we are so quick to forget
what comes to us at this point.

This is the simplest exercise to get rid of worries,
solve problems and increase creativity and joy.

Be prepared with suggestions if you want to have something specific in mind for this exercise, or just let your mind come up with what comes.

Repeat daily for several days.
Practice makes perfect.

When you start using this,
you feel how powerful the mind is
and always wants the best for us

Unbelievable but true.

Chapter 13

Betty Erickson's Self-Hypnosis

This technique was developed by Betty Erickson, who was the wife of Dr. Milton Erickson. Betty had a great understanding and interest in how sight, hearing, and moving images in the mind affect our mental world and relaxation.

This method used by Betty is an excellent method, which has become very popular all over the world.
It's very good for releasing stress and achieving peace of mind.
It exists in several versions, but here comes one of them.

Before you start the process into self-hypnosis, it is good to have the goal you are going to work with clearly in mind. It is also very good to write down the goal and the suggestions you are going to say to yourself during the

self-hypnosis. Keep the suggestions in as few words as possible. Have them in present tense and positive.
Goals are about what you are aiming for in your life.
Where do you want to see the changes, and how do you want these changes to be?
Use your imagination and visualize this clearly.
Review the suggestions you want to use while in the hypnotic state. Remember that all suggestions must be positive and in the present tense.

In self-hypnosis, you can use your mind only and not use any recording if you want to.

Follow the script below, and you will see how it is done.

You need to relax your mind.

First, work with your eyes open.
Take a moment after you read each sentence
to give yourself time to think about the answer in your mind.
Then, close your eyes and repeat it with your eyes closed.
When you get there,
you can open your eyes and read your suggestions.
Repeat several times or remember the suggestions
and work on them in your mind.
Then go back slowly into relaxation again
and let your mind process these suggestions.
Let yourself see this as clearly as you can.

When coming back from self-hypnosis,
Count from 1 to 5 slowly

When you're ready, follow these steps:

Betty Erickson, self-hypnosis

Find a comfortable place to stay.
Allow yourself to relax
both mind and body
and feel the relaxation come to you.

Stare at a certain spot on the wall,
and don't move away from that spot for a while.

Notice 3 things you see.
Do not move your eyes from the point.
They can be objects or shadows,
A chair, table, lamp, refraction, etc.

Notice 3 things you hear.
Your breath, the wind outside,
people around you,
the sound of a car, an airplane...
some sound outside or inside.

Notice 3 things you feel.
The chair you're sitting on,
your clothes,
your feet on the floor,

your hands, etc.

Notice 2 things you see.
Notice 2 things you hear.
Notice 2 things you feel.

Notice 1 thing you see.
Notice 1 thing you hear.
Notice 1 thing you feel.

Now close your eyes
and let your imagination help you.

Visualize 3 things you perceive (in your mind).
Visualize 3 things you hear.
Visualize 3 things you feel.

Visualize 2 things that you perceive (in your mind).
Visualize 2 things you hear.
Visualize 2 things you feel.
Visualize 1 thing that you perceive (in your mind).
Visualize 1 thing you hear.
Visualize 1 thing you feel.

Now you are in a very good state of self-hypnosis relaxation,
and you are ready to start working with your mind.

You can open your eyes
and read your goals and the suggestions

you had written on the paper earlier.
You can also just let your mind go
to your goals and find new ways to a solution.
Or if you make a recording on your phone,
you can put your goals into the recording
and listen.

Allow yourself to go inward
and feel the relaxation.
It is a calm and peaceful situation.

In this deep state of relaxation,
you can give yourself suggestions or simply relax.
You can put into effect
the suggestions you had in mind
before you started this self- hypnosis.
Simply trust your mind to let the suggestions flow.
The more you can let go
and let your mind flow,
he easier it will be for your suggestions
to take root within you.

Repeat your suggestions several times.

Visualize the suggestions that you have achieved
and find out how you feel about them.
Give yourself a moment
so, your mind can visualize
and your imagination can work for you.
When you are ready,

you can either open your eyes
and come back out of hypnosis,
or you can count from 1 to 5
and come back at your own pace.

When you come back from hypnosis,
you are wide awake
with great energy and are full of joy,
and totally ready to do something exciting.

This method can also be used to help others

This method can also be used
when trying to get someone to calm down.
You can sit opposite each other
and ask questions in turn.

No 1 3 things you see (no2 answer)
No 2 3 things you see (no1 answer) and so on
No 1 3 things you hear
No 2 3 things you hear
No 1 3 things you feel
No 2 3 things you feel
No 1 2 things you see
No 2 2 things you see
No 1 2 things you hear
No 2 2 things you hear
No 1 2 things you feel
No 2 2 things you feel
No 1 1 item you see
No 2 1 item you see

No 1 1 thing you hear
No 2 1 thing you hear
No 1 1 thing you feel
No 2 1 thing you feel

Close your eyes and repeat this again.
See, hear, and feel x3 – x2 – x1 alternating.

Already there?
Then you are in a state of great stillness and peace.
And there you can start working with your mind
or continue with your suggestions.
Or simply allow yourself to relax for a while
and enjoy the quietness.
When you are ready,
you can come back from hypnosis.
Either simply open your eyes
and come back from self-hypnosis
or count from 1 to 5 and come back that way
refreshed and in a great state of well-being and optimism.

Please try this method. It is so nice to find out how easy it is and how well it works.

Chapter 14

The Final Chapter

How are you going to use this book?

Now it's the last chapter of this book, so it is time to start creating your own self-hypnosis.
What is it that you want to deal with in your own mind?

In this book, we have covered what is hypnosis and what is self-hypnosis, and how we can use these techniques to improve our lives.

This book also teaches how you can record your own self-hypnosis script the way you want it and then how you can listen to it when it suits you.

Check out the self-hypnosis scripts in this book and find what works for you. Create your own script.

Write your hypnosis script on a piece of paper so you have it in front of you to read aloud.
Then, find the phone and create your recording.

Self-hypnosis can be done in many ways.

- It is possible to use only the mind and systematically go into self-hypnosis.
- You can record your own self-hypnosis on your phone and listen at your convenience.
- You can listen to other people's recordings that you can download online or buy.

Many people like to start using a self-hypnosis script and read it into their phone and listen that way.

Self-hypnosis needs to be practiced and repeated over and over again to achieve good skills. But it will come very soon.

There are more and more people using self-hypnosis in today's world. But self-hypnosis has been used for centuries.

There are a lot of athletes, actors, musicians, and just regular people who use self-hypnosis to get better at what they are doing, improve focus, manage anxiety, and increase performance.

Tiger Woods

The famous golfer used and still uses self-hypnosis in his daily life.

He uses self-hypnosis to visualize each swing and each shot in his mind before hitting the ball. He also uses self-hypnosis to get himself in the right frame of mind for each game.

Self-hypnosis has helped him, like so many other great athletes, to calm his mind, release anxiety, and become 100 percent focused when playing.

Brandi Chastain

The American soccer player used self-hypnosis when she won the gold medal in the 2014 Olympics. She still uses self-hypnosis and talks about the importance of preparation, being positive and optimistic, envisioning how you want things to be, and believing that you can do that. Then everything goes much better.

They used self-hypnosis and visualized every stroke or scenario. These strategies were necessary to prepare for victory and, in their cases, win big victories.

Michael Jordan

A famous former professional basketball player used self-hypnosis before every game to increase his mental stamina. Chicago Bulls and LA Lakers coach Phil Jackson said the Bulls practiced hypnosis daily as he coached them to six NBA championships.

Adele

The singer and songwriter has used self-hypnosis to overcome stage fright and anxiety. The stage fright is invisible, but people noticed the results when she lost weight after hypnotherapy. Her success has greatly influenced the image of hypnosis (Hughes, 2021).

Matt Damon,

actor and screenwriter, stopped smoking with the help of hypnosis.

Kate Middleton,

wife of William, Prince of Wales, used self-hypnosis to reduce and get rid of morning sickness during pregnancy. She also used hypnobirthing when she gave birth to her children and was very happy with that method.

Albert Einstein

used self-hypnosis daily. Always in the afternoon every day. He used hypnosis to explore his creativity. His theory of relativity came to him when he was in a trance, he said himself.

Thomas Edison

practiced self-hypnosis. See Chapter 12.

Edison believed that in this state, where you are between sleep and wakefulness, you are especially open to creative thinking and problem-solving. He used this method to tap into his subconscious mind and create new ideas for his inventions.

This is a very interesting aspect of Edison's working habits.

Norman Vincent Peale

was a pastor in New York. He wrote many books on how we can influence our well-being by controlling our thoughts because thought is a great energy, and thoughts have a great influence on how we feel.

When I was a teenager, there was one book I really liked, and it was called The Power of Positive Thinking. It was first published in 1952. This book has been republished again and again as it is still widely read. Peale wrote about how positivity and thoughts have a big impact on how we do things and how we feel.

We can have such a great impact on our well-being by learning to talk nicely to ourselves and find peace in our minds.

The Power of Positive Thinking covers how to break free from this eternal self-criticism and self-doubt.

He also talks in the book about how you can get rid of worry, anxiety, and frustration. He points out that positive thoughts can change a lot and improve life in many ways.

Some quotes from Norman Vincent Peale:

"Get up against your obstacles and do something about them. You'll find they don't have half the strength you think they do."
"Change your thoughts, and you change your world."

"Repetition of the same thought or physical action develops into a habit if it is repeated often enough and thus becomes an involuntary response."

Dale Carnegie
was a salesman and trained actor. Later in life, he began to teach expression and communication. He created the Dale Carnegie courses on communication, which are and have been in demand all over the world. These courses are still taught and are well attended because of how great they are.

He wrote many books, but the most famous of them is How to Stop Worrying and Start Living, which was published for the first time in 1948.

This book has sold over seven million copies and has helped millions of people overcome worry and anxiety. Techniques in the book teach ways to get rid of worry and anxiety.

Some quotes from Dale Carnegie:

"Let's fill our minds with thoughts of peace, courage, health, and hope, for our life is what our thoughts make it."

"If you can't sleep, then get up and do something instead of lying there worrying. It's the worry that gets you, not the lack of sleep."

"Happiness doesn't depend on any external conditions it is governed by our mental attitude."

"Unjust criticism is usually a disguised compliment. It often means that you have aroused jealousy or envy."

Dale Carnegie and Norman Vincent Peale were friends, and when you read their books, you see that they sometimes cite the same stories or experiences.

Why do I mention these books here?

It's because I feel strongly that these books are related to self-hypnosis, where we also use a positive mind and visualize in our mind how we want to achieve our goals. And we want to talk to ourselves nicely, be constructive, and keep our thoughts positive. Then everything goes much better.

These books discuss all these techniques, and I encourage you to check them out. They are really worth it.

It is possible to work toward your goals and desires through self-hypnosis. Visualize yourself in your mind where you want to be and let your imagination take you there. Once you have this clear vision in mind, you are on track with your goals.

How do you want your life to be?

If you had a magic wand and could change what you want to change, what would you change and fix in your mind?

Self-hypnosis isn't a cure-all, and you can't make a bone fracture heal faster with self-hypnosis, but it is possible to allow yourself to feel better in any given situation. That's a big deal. The mind is so powerful.

There is so much power within you that you can use to make yourself feel good. For example, you can choose to be happy, and that positivity will spread to those around you.

Good luck using self-hypnosis to improve your life and well-being, improve your athletic and work skills, and increase your confidence to do what you want to do.

You can do so many things by controlling your mind. Practice makes perfect.

Good luck to you.

BIBLIOGRAPHY

Carnegie, Dale. How to Stop Worrying and Start Living. Simon and Schuster, 1948.

Hughes, Paul. "Adele, Oscars, Anxiety, and Hypnotherapy." Resolved Hypnotherapy, 2021.

Peale, Norman, Vincent. The Power of Positive Thinking. Prentice Hall, 1952.

Rees, Mathieu. "What to Know About Self-Hypnosis." Medical News Today, 2023. https://www.medicalnewstoday.com/articles/self-hypnosis

Nongard, Richard, K. Panoramic Dream Analysis: A Step-by-Step Guide to Discovering the True Meaning of Your Dreams. Subliminal Science Press, 2023.

The Seven Most Effective Methods of Self-Hypnosis: How to Create Rapid Change in Your Health, Wealth, and Habits. Independently published, 2019.

www.ingramcontent.com/pod-product-compliance
Lightning Source LLC
LaVergne TN
LVHW041216150826
845673LV00001B/421
* 9 7 8 9 9 3 5 9 0 8 7 6 6 *